"Finding your sweet spot . . . Discovering your ⸻ calling. These are the sought-for concepts that burn deep in all of us. They begin early, and they nag at us until the very end. Colin's book *Crossroads* is the driver's manual for that journey. Get this book. Read this book. Follow this book."

STEPHEN R. GRAVES, founder, Coaching by Cornerstone

"Colin Creel once again weaves together faithful application of God's Word and the 'seasoned' advice of ancient and modern leaders in a way that speaks to the heart of the reader. We long to sense God's calling, and Colin helps us take that step of faith along and journey into the unknown. Great reading for the young as they embark on their 'careers' and for others further along the path who find that once again transitions, life changes, bring that deep desire to question and fully embrace God's call on their lives."

EVAN HUNTER, Director, Ivy Jungle Network

"I believe that God has designed each of us with a purpose. In *Crossroads: Navigating Your Calling and Career,* Colin Creel provides refreshing, real-world wisdom that will help you discern God's will for your life. Don't miss this opportunity."

John Smoltz, Atlanta Braves pitcher

"Colin Creel is a godly man with important things to say to our generation. We are a group that desperately needs sound teaching on God's 'calling,' and Colin is someone to listen to."

MATT LUTZ, actor (*End of the Spear; A Walk To Remember*)

"Have you ever questioned the difference between your purpose in life and your calling from God? Have you ever questioned if you are growing or wasting time working in the area you're in? If so, question no longer. This Scripture-filled, expertly documented, practical book is ready to give you answers and information. Colin Creel makes sure you can understand the difference. Read and learn."

THELMA WELLS, President, A Woman of God Ministries;
Founder, Daughters of Zion Leadership Mentoring Program;
speaker/author, Women of Faith Conferences

"When I was just out of college and trying to figure out what I was 'supposed' to do with my career, I clumsily tried to seek advice from those who were more experienced. I wish I had had a resource like this at the time! Colin's book not only provides great encouragement to make the most of our marketplace callings—it allows readers to 'listen in' on conversations with seasoned professionals who have some terrific insights to share."

SHAUNTI FELDHAHN, best-selling author, public speaker, and
nationally syndicated newspaper columnist

"There's a lot in this book that modernity has either ignored or discounted, including common sense rooted in spiritual soil! Colin understands the importance of God's call in one's life, and how that same call can not only set forth a career but sustain that career when it's going against some of life's toughest winds. The sweet aroma of this book will last long after its covers have been shut. This is some good reading about how good decisions can deliver a good life to those who will take time to hear God's voice and obey!"

JOHN D. HULL, president/CEO, EQUIP/ISS

"Colin Creel's *Crossroads* is a clearly written, practical, and biblically based guidebook to both calling and career. The book is rich in anecdotes and illustrations from his own experience and that of many others, and it offers seasoned advice and points to ponder throughout. The discussion of the various facets of career is a vivid portrait of discipleship in action."

KENNETH BOA, President, Reflections Ministries, Atlanta;
President, Trinity House Publishers, Atlanta

"This excellent book not only leads you to the 'crossroads,' it provides a map that can provide direction for answering the most important questions in life. People who are able to align their career choices with their God-given calling are destined for a life of meaning and joy. Those who honestly confront the 'Points to Ponder' at the end of each chapter will receive a priceless gift of purpose and direction!"

BOB FISHER, President, Belmont University; coauthor,
Real Dream Teams and (forthcoming) *Conversations with the
Soon Departed: What Really Matters*

"At Wake Forest Colin Creel distinguished himself as a leader in Chi Rho, our Christian men's a cappella group, and as a counselor to students and parents in our Admissions Office. As an author, teacher, administrator, and coach, he continues to provide wise counsel based on a profound and well-examined faith. This newest book is particularly useful for those who are discerning their calling. While it is addressed to those in their twenties, people of all generations can benefit from the wisdom and struggles Colin shares."

THOMAS K. HEARN JR., President Emeritus, Wake Forest University

CROSSROADS

NAVIGATING YOUR
CALLING AND CAREER

COLIN CREEL

CROSSWAY BOOKS
WHEATON, ILLINOIS

Crossroads

Copyright © 2008 by Colin Creel

Published by Crossway Books
        a publishing ministry of Good News Publishers
        1300 Crescent Street
        Wheaton, Illinois 60187

Cover design: Josh Dennis

Cover illustration: Veer & iStock

First printing, 2008

Printed in the United States of America

Library of Congress Cataloging-in-Publication Data
Creel, Colin, 1974–
   Crossroads : navigating your calling and career / Colin Creel.
      p. cm.
   Includes index.
   ISBN 978-1-58134-952-8 (tpb)
   1. Work—Religious aspects—Christianity. 2. Work—Biblical Teaching.
I. Title.
BT738.5.C74   2007
248.4—dc22   2007029556

VP		18	17	16	15	14	13	12	11	10	09	08
15	14	13	12	11	10	9	8	7	6	5	4	3	2	1

To my Class of 2006 Bible Study

Ben, Brandon, Bret, Brett,
Jake, Jason (coleader), Justin, Mark,
Matt, Peter, Steven, Taylor, TJ, Tommy, Will

*May this book help you find your way
as much as you helped me find mine.*

CONTENTS

FOREWORD

Are you prepared for a journey that just may change your entire view on life as you know it? That is exactly the adventure you are about to embark upon. Colin Creel has taken real-life experiences from today as well as from thousands of years ago to reveal the truth about our careers, callings, and what to do if you are just getting started!

The world is full of false information and flat-out lies when it comes to success and "making your mark" in life. Colin, through the Word of God and his own personal experiences, counteracts those lies in a powerful way to display the truth and hope that is so vital for our day-to-day living. Each chapter is designed to reach into the corners of your mind and help you examine your perspectives and take action to align them with the mind-set of Christ. At the end of each chapter, discussion questions will help generate your own personal thoughts.

I talk to hundreds of teenagers, college students, and even adults who are wondering what in the world they are doing here and where God wants them to be! According to the messages of the world and the media, we are supposed to have it all figured out by the time we graduate from high school or at the latest college graduation day. School prepares a student for knowledge of a certain job, but what about the day-in and day-out questions of life?

No matter what age you are or what stage of life you are in, this book will help. Colin Creel is tackling some of the hardest questions we ask in life. He has gathered wisdom from Scripture and uses interviews with older men and women who are leading the way as well as his own encounters. You may be perfectly satisfied with your job but find yourself asking what will come next or wondering if you are making a difference. Allow each chapter to help mold your decisions and the path down which you are heading. Watch out—it may just challenge you to make a 180-degree turn and accept the calling for which you were made! It's always a thrill to open the gate and take the first step on a path that has never seen mankind before. That is what this book will be like for many of you. You will take in sights and smells that you have never considered possible. Grab your walking stick and a notebook for your thoughts—this is going to be one life-changing trip!

Joe White
President, Kanakuk Kamps

INTRODUCTION

As my last year of college came to a close, I found myself standing in Mike's driveway. Like so many college seniors, I felt unsure about what was next while simultaneously being exhilarated by the thought of charting my own course. Mike Edens led a Bible study for a group of my friends our junior and senior years. His steadfast spirit served as a beacon of wisdom in a confusing time. We stood in his driveway for a while that afternoon. In many ways that time was a crossroads in my life. During our time together Mike offered one of the greatest compliments I have ever received. He said, "Colin, however you define success, you will achieve it." I still wrestle with this question of *success*. I hoped and prayed that my life would clearly mirror my definition of success, but would it? If someone followed me around for weeks at a time, what would they see? How we define success serves as a critical question in our journey because it drives many into careers they loathe while others meet life where it meets them, in their sweet spots.

Unlike many peers, I enjoy what I do. Over the past few years, though, I have begun to question where I am and to ask myself what's next. Like so many others, I, too, fall into the traps of promises of financial gain and influence. I am always processing life, at times to a fault. Balancing being prepared to meet a credential-laden society while at the same time not being driven by it proves challenging. Society tells us to keep climbing up the ladder of success, but what if you feel fulfilled on the rung where you currently reside?

After writing my first book, *Perspectives*, many individuals told me they desired for me to go deeper into the whole notion of one's career. This book seeks to help you navigate the murky waters of career and calling by looking at the biblical view of calling, offering practical guidelines within your career, and recognizing that each of us is here on this earth for a reason. None of us is here by accident, and there are no accidental occupations. There are no hierarchies in occupations either; rather, it is important for you to pursue whatever talents and gifts the Lord has afforded you.

As a thirty-three-year-old Christian who has sought God's leading in making many of the above decisions, I have set out to share both what I have learned on my journey as well as the advice of some older, wiser men and women who can look back with discernment regarding the life-molding decisions all of us face. This book has many different angles—my writings, excerpts from Christian literature, business examples, life experiences, and interviews. Essentially I went about the task of asking more seasoned individuals the following questions:

- What steps led to your current vocation/calling?
- What do you wish you had known as you began your career/vocation?
- What advice would you offer the next generation?
- What were your biggest challenges early in your career, and what helped or hindered you from overcoming these challenges?

By no means have I unearthed the Holy Grail, but this book will help anyone who ever asked themselves any of the following questions:

INTRODUCTION

- Am I in the right job?
- Is it time to move on?
- How can I find more joy in my job?
- How can I keep my job while maintaining my integrity?
- How can I balance work and my home life?

A special word of thanks goes to my headmaster Zach Young, who entered into a conversation a few years ago with me that served as the impetus for this book, as well as Don Flow, who shared his insights over a long lunch. Thank you to the late Bill Starling, my first real boss, who taught me a great deal about life. Thank you also to *Relevant Magazine*, specifically Cameron Strang, for taking a chance on an unknown author by publishing *Perspectives*, which eventually led to Crossway signing me for this book, and to Jill Carter, Ted Griffin, Josh Dennis, and Allan Fisher, who have been wonderfully responsive and helpful in crafting this book. My agent, Leslie Nunn Reed, has been gracious in assisting me through the genesis of this book, and Bible Gateway's excellent online Scripture reference system has helped me find verses when I could only remember small portions. Thank you to Joe White for his joyful willingness to write the foreword.

Intellectually, Evan Hunter and my department chair, Russ Custer, continually push me to see the world through a different set of lenses. Professionally, Joel Vaughn, Bob Mills, Kyle Chowning, Cara Davis, Margaret Feinberg, Susan Yates, Jeff Jackson, Heidi Lloyd (photographer), Laura Lloyd, Dr. Stephen Graves, and Ashby Foltz (web designer) all provided wonderful guidance along the way. A very special thank you to Kendra Morris, my in-house editor at Wesleyan School, who put up with me all summer as I would appear mysteriously at her doorstep with chapters in hand, desperately in need of revision, and to Mark and Steven for their research assistance. Thank you also to the Wesleyan, Wake Forest, and John Burroughs communities for their endless support and encouragement. In addition, thank you to the Barclays and Flows for never giving up on me. Finally, I thank my parents, in-laws, and grandparents for instilling in me an enduring work ethic, my sister for supporting me, and my wonderful wife, Krista, who was not mad at me when I failed to dedicate this book to her.

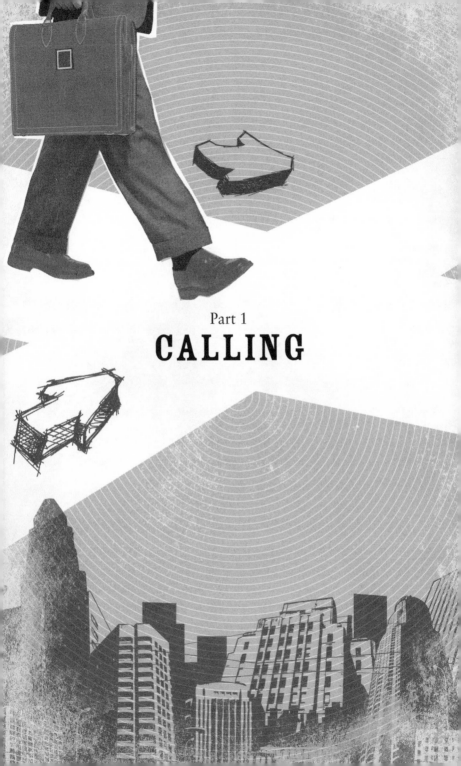

Part 1
CALLING

CALLING—A DEFINITION

When I hear the word *call* or *calling*, many different ideas scatter across my mind. Thus, for the purpose of clarity, allow me to elaborate on the component of the call that will serve as the focal point in this book. Most scholars agree that the call of God contains at least two primary arms and perhaps three arms. R. Paul Stevens suggests the three-components option: "the call to belong to God, the call to be God's people in life, and the call to do God's work."[1] Os Guinness collapses Stevens's second and third callings into one: "our secondary calling, considering who God is as sovereign, is that everyone, everywhere, and in everything should think, speak, live and act entirely for him. We can therefore properly say as a matter of secondary calling that we are called to homemaking or to the practice of law or to art history."[2] In other words, as long as you are serving Christ in your thoughts, your words, and your actions, your secondary calling takes all shapes and sizes depending on your affinities, abilities, and opportunities (which will be discussed in a later chapter).

As Christians our primary calling is "to belong to God." We are called to be God's people on this earth. Guinness says, "We are called to someone (God), not to something (such as motherhood, politics, or teaching) or to somewhere (such as the inner city or Outer Mongolia)."[3] This calling focuses on our discipleship and on the fact that "the promise is for you and your children and for all who are far off—for all whom the Lord our God will call" (Acts 2:39). As children of God, we understand that we are works in progress with feet of clay and that we continually need to "press on toward the goal to win the prize for which God has called [us] heavenward in Christ Jesus" (Philippians 3:14). Our secondary callings only have meaning because we have a primary calling. There is only one primary calling for Christians, whereas there are potentially many secondary callings for each of us. For instance, I am called to be a teacher, a coach, a writer, a husband, and hopefully someday a father. These secondary callings may change throughout your lifetime. For instance, while I was in college my secondary calling was first and foremost to honor God in my academics. Too often I fell short of that goal, but it was a goal nonetheless.

Most people find some secondary callings that will never change throughout their lifetime regardless of their situations or surroundings. For example, my friend Charlie is a teacher at heart. Even though he is currently pursuing his Master's in church history, he always takes a great deal of pride and thoroughness to ensure that others understand whatever he is teaching, whether it's the rules to a new game or how to find a certain restaurant. Our primary calling is "to belong to God," and our secondary callings are more commonly referred to as our "work."

Historically, the term *calling* is often misused. My friend Andrew Boyd would say he is *called* into the ministry of Young Life, which is certainly true as evidenced by his accompanying gifts and affirmation from all who know him. But if my friend Jimbo were to say he was *called* into finance because of his analytical mind, those same people who nodded their head in affirmation for Andrew would smirk at Jimbo. Why? There is an underlying assumption that calling only occurs within the clergy, and in addition most presuppose a hierarchy of callings; to be officially *called,* you must be in "full-time ministry." Throughout my life many close to me have often questioned why I am not a pastor, or in other words why I have not chosen to serve in "full-time ministry." A long-time friend and mentor, Jim Reed, once said to me, "If you can do anything else, then do not go into traditional full-time ministry." These wise words have guided me through the years.

I remember early in my life questioning my devotion to God because I never had a strong desire to serve a church in an official capacity. The truth is, the world needs godly men and women to work in all fields in order to reweave *shalom,* God's vision for a flourishing city here on earth. Our work on this earth "is not something we do apart from God, as the secular worker would view it. Work is not something beneath God's dignity or concern as the Two-Story view believes. Nor is work a game that we play with non-Christians in order to accomplish a more important agenda, as the Mainstream advocate holds."[4]

This book seeks to clarify a biblical view of our secondary calling, to explore how we are called, as well as to offer practical guidelines to seizing the opportunities your secondary callings afford you. None of us is an ordinary person, and there are no ordinary occupations. We need to dispense our notions of hierarchical callings and embrace our God-ordained wiring in order to contribute to the kingdom. "Jesus built the kingdom as a carpenter before he built it as a rabbi. And he taught us in the parable of the talents that the question for disciples is not which callings they have but how faithfully they pursue them."[5]

SEASONED ADVICE

Dennis Bakke, sixty-one; president and CEO, Imagine Schools; chairman emeritus, The AES Corporation; author of New York

CALLING

Times *bestseller*, Joy at Work: A Revolutionary Approach to Fun on the Job; *www.dennisbakke.com*; *Arlington, VA:*

Miss McInnes, a petite woman in her early 50s, was my math teacher from 8th to 11th grade. Polio had left her with a withered arm, but her brilliance and dedication were her most important features. During my senior year, I decided to stay at school before home football games, which were played on Friday nights, instead of spending an hour and a half riding the bus home and then turning right around to get back in time for the game. Miss McInnes invited me to have supper with her before those games at the local cafe about a quarter of a mile from school. One evening she asked the question put to every high school senior: "What are you going to do with your life?" I gave her my usual answer: "I don't really have any idea, although I am hoping to go to college." I thought the college answer would bear out the faith she had shown in me. Fewer than 40 percent of my classmates planned to attend college. "I have some advice for you," she responded without hesitation. "Raymond and Lowell [my older and younger brothers, respectively, both of whom had scrupulously avoided taking math from her] have already committed to be pastors. Someone needs to support them."

To my knowledge, Miss McInnes was not a churchgoer or an amateur theologian. But her advice to me captured what I had been taught about the purpose of work and God's attitude toward it. The best occupation for a devout Christian, according to the teachings of my church, was to be a missionary, preferably in rural Africa. My cousin Gordon Bakke filled that role for over 20 years. Second best was to be a pastor or priest. My brothers were called to this kind of work. Third in the hierarchy were the "helping" professions: teachers, social workers, nurses, and others who served in similar ways, especially those who were not paid high salaries. People seemed to get more credit if they performed these kinds of jobs within a Christian-based organization, rather than working for the government, a public school, or a profit-making organization. Next in line was government work. Homemaking was a respected occupation as well. At the bottom were commercial and business jobs such as secretaries, technicians, factory workers, and executives. The primary path to redemption for these unfortunate souls was to make enough money to support those working in "full-time Christian ministry." They could also atone by volunteering their time to do something significant for the local church or another Christian activity when not at their jobs. Miss McInnes had advised me to use my talents to play the role dictated by my religious beliefs, at least to the extent that I understood them at the time.

One of my core beliefs, then and now, is that every entity incorporated by the state should serve the needs of society in an ethical and economically healthy manner. The same goal is appropriate for both profit-making and not-for-profit business organizations. My views on this point are based on biblical principles, starting with the Creation story in the Bible.

The Creation story begins with God working. He is creating the universe. He then creates mankind in His own image. He assigned humans to manage the Earth and all the animals, plants, and other resources it contained. God gave us the capability and authority to work. Through the act of Creation, He showed us how to undertake this responsibility. Genesis 2:5 says, ". . . and there was not a man to till the ground." This implies that one of the reasons mankind exists is to work.

Work itself was not the goal of life. We were not placed in the Garden purely to work. The Bible says that we were created to have a relationship with God and to honor Him. Work is one of the ways we honor or "glorify" God. Humankind's first important job description was to manage the Earth and all that comes from God's creation. I believe this includes the ideas, services, and products that come from the imaginations of people. We honor God by furthering His creation. Work should be an act of worship to God. God is pleased when people steward their talents and energy to achieve these ends.

The Bible does not appear to give priorities to the various kinds of stewardship or work. All kinds of production and management activities honor God. If the work is seen by the worker as something accomplished for God and meeting a need in society, it is pleasing to God. Some roles that modern society tends to see as less valuable and mundane—animal husbandry and tilling the soil, for instance—are specifically mentioned as worthy endeavors in the Garden. Isn't it logical that all work that results in food, clothing, shelter, rest or recreation, beauty, and a host of other worthy ends can be acts of worship to God and seen as valuable contributions to society? Are these not activities that can be as sacred as rearing children, teaching school, or even carrying out priestly duties?

Though I often fail to live up to God's highest standards, I realize that my approach to the job is consistent with the expectation God places on all my daily work. God does not differentiate among types of work. Halfhearted efforts and sloppy work do not honor God. He expects me to use my best efforts, talents, and skills in every task I undertake, whatever its importance.

(From *Joy at Work* (Seattle: PVG, 2006), used by permission.)

POINTS TO PONDER

1. How does Os Guinness's definition of calling align with yours? "Calling is the truth that God calls us to himself so decisively that everything we are, everything we do, and everything we have is invested with a special devotion and dynamism lived out as a response to his summons and service."[6]

2. Read Matthew 28:16–20.

3. How does this passage align with our calling?

NOTES

1. R. Paul Stevens, *The Other Six Days* (Grand Rapids, MI: Eerdmans, 1999), p. 88.

2. Os Guinness, *The Call* (Nashville: Word, 1998), p. 31.

3. Ibid.

4. Douglas Sherman and William Hendricks, *Your Work Matters to God* (Colorado Springs: NavPress, 1987), p. 77.

5. Cornelius Plantinga Jr., *Engaging God's World: A Christian Vision of Faith, Learning, and Living* (Grand Rapids, MI: Eerdmans, 2002), p. 121.

6. Guinness, *The Call*, p. 4.

WORK IS A GIFT

Work is a gift from God. God granted work before the Fall, but too often I hear people refer to work as a curse as a result of the Fall. Work is not a curse; it is a gift from God in order to join Him in serving as stewards of His land. But like all things after the Fall, work is tainted as a result of our sin. In the beginning God "took the man and put him in the Garden of Eden to work it and take care of it" (Genesis 2:15). This verse occurs prior to Eve's creation and both Adam's and Eve's decisions to sin. God saw that Adam was lonely and tried to find a suitable helper for him by bringing "all the beasts of the field and all the birds of the air . . . to the man to see what he would name them; and whatever the man called each living creature, that was its name. So the man gave names to all the livestock, the birds of the air and all the beasts of the field" (Genesis 2:19–20).

When I reflect on Adam's naming all of God's creation, I don't usually stop to think how long that must have taken him. But think about it for a moment—*all* of God's creations. As a writer I try to use different words to describe situations or items, but inevitably I fall back to my old standards. Imagine Adam sitting on a rock while all of these creatures paraded past him. His job included creating names from a new language that served as good descriptors for the various creatures. I wonder what he thought the first time he saw a platypus!

After naming all of the creatures, Adam did not find a suitable helper; so God made woman. Eventually Satan, in the form of a snake, convinced Eve to eat the fruit from the forbidden tree, and Adam followed her example. As a result of their sin, the Lord cursed Satan (Genesis 3:14–15), the woman who would experience pain during childbirth and allow her husband to rule over her (Genesis 3:16), and Adam as God cursed the ground and made his days on earth finite (Genesis 3:17–19). Nowhere in God's punishments does He curse work. This distinction might seem small, but, for instance, in Genesis 3:17 God says, "Cursed is the ground because of you; through painful toil you will eat of it all the days of your life." God cursed the ground. Work became harder for us, but he never cursed work. I personally cannot imagine a life without work. Work helps give a person purpose and a sense of fulfillment, assuming we are performing tasks in line with our gifts and abilities.

In a recent issue of *Fortune* magazine, Lee Iacocca, former auto industry tycoon, was asked his secret to a fulfilling retirement. He responded, "If you don't stay engaged, it hurts you physiologically. A couple of my bosses at Ford retired at 65, and they went home to die. They were dead by the time they were 68. They had no interests. When you atrophy, you die. Retirement isn't the end; it is the beginning."[1] Articles on retirement are flooding nearly every magazine lately for a variety of reasons, but mainly because the baby-boomer generation has crossed over into retirement. The picture of American retirement always includes moving someplace warm and indulging in one's hobbies. Retirement for most, especially driven people, proves extremely difficult because human beings were created in part to work. Many of these articles address retirees' going back into the workforce after officially retiring because of their desire to stay engaged. Both of my parents, who are retirement age, continue to work part-time. We all desire to feel as though we are contributing to society in some way. Authors Doug Sherman and William Hendricks suggest, "If God had wanted to punish man through work, the best thing He could have done would have been to take away man's work entirely."[2] No wonder so many retirees or lottery winners are clinically depressed! Sitting back and sipping margaritas in our golden years was never God's plan.

In the beginning God created everything, and then sin entered the world and infected everything. However, "God redeems all things through Jesus Christ. Christians, like the Christ whose name they bear, share in God's redemptive and creative purposes in all things. Therefore Christian vocation includes all aspects of cultural and social life."[3] Our work, or our secondary calling, serves as an instrumental vehicle to redeem the world culturally and socially. Our work and our ministries are not two separate entities. Unfortunately, even within the Christian culture there is often a bifurcation between work and one's spiritual life. *Christianity Today* carried a great interview of Dennis Bakke, the author of *Joy at Work*. The interviewer asked Bakke how CEOs responded to his book. He said most Christian CEOs "have bought into the idea of a segmented society, and they would like to protect employees rather than free them. They want to be nice to them, and treat them, they say, with dignity. They tend to live out their faith in terms of personal piety. But they don't understand the implications of falling into the Industrial Revolution trap of structuring a workplace."[4] As Bakke suggests, we need to be free to use our talents. We need to be free to play our role in God's redemptive work in the world. Man is made to work; it is God's gift to us. God knows we will only be truly fulfilled when we align our skills, talents, passions, and experiences in order to partner with Him.

SEASONED ADVICE

Jim Stephenson, fifty-six; president of Yancey Bros. Co., "The Nation's Oldest Caterpillar Dealer," Atlanta:

By the time I graduated law school, I had worked in over twenty-five different jobs ranging from chopping cotton to digging ditches, serving as a waiter, bartending, selling encyclopedias, clothing sales, telemarketing, working on loading docks, dishwashing, and driving the Mr. Softee Ice Cream truck to name a few. Believe it or not, driving that ice cream truck was the most dangerous. I looked like a cash box on wheels evidenced by my ability to get held up more than once. After law school, I joined a law firm for eighteen years. Early on in my marriage, my father-in-law, who owned Yancey Bros. Co., asked me if I desired to work for the business. At that point in our lives, I did not feel it was the wisest decision for our marriage even though it was a wonderful opportunity. A few years later, her dad sold the business to his brother who had three sons. There were many times during my legal career that I second-guessed myself about that decision.

As it turns out, I was given an opportunity not just to join but to buy the company in 1994. We borrowed more money than I thought anyone would ever loan us and bought it. The local economy has been very good over the last decade, and we have grown our company from four hundred to twelve hundred employees. I am confident now that I made the right decision. One of our seasoned service managers once told me, "At the end of the day, you cannot look back; the past is immovable and unchangeable, so turn forward." Even though I stayed with the same law firm for eighteen years, I would encourage those beginning their career to not fear calculated risks. Unless you are positive you are in the right place, feel free to explore other possibilities. The culture in which you work is of paramount importance. Your personal fit within your company's culture will have a huge impact on your happiness. Early on in my career I did not understand how much institutional commitment to core values varies from corporation to corporation. Nor did I understand the extent to which that commitment and those values drive employee satisfaction. I strongly suggest that every job applicant interviewing with a new prospective employer should ask to know the company's core values. If the interviewer doesn't know or is not comfortable discussing this subject, that speaks volumes about the culture of that company and your prospects for fitting in.

Everything we do at Yancey Bros. Co. is tied to our core values, like integrity, commitment to excellence, and a strong customer focus. We hire people based on whether or not they are a good fit with our values. One employee once told me, "I'm not going to work; I'm going to my other family." We believe so strongly in creating a positive working culture that every three months all of our employees fill out a satisfaction survey ranging from the safety of the working environment to feeling comfortable about offering improvement suggestions. There's a climate of trust surrounding the survey. Trust that our employees will be honest. Trust that the management will actively improve areas with low scores. This past quarter, numbers were the highest in company history, 88 percent highly positive, up from 76 percent in 2000.

We're serious about people and making Yancey a great place for people to work. We're all responsible for this place in which we work. I may not know how to build a tractor, repair a tractor, or sell a tractor, but I am responsible for making this place a work environment they feel good about as they drive to work in the morning and proud of what they did as they drive home at the end of the day. Hopefully, I'm doing my part in making a difference in the lives of others. Looking back, the goals I set for myself in my youth (raise a son, write a book, and play Augusta National) weren't high enough, so now I'm working toward some new goals: growing a truly great corporate culture at Yancey Bros. Co. and making a really positive difference in the lives of everybody who works there.

POINTS TO PONDER

1. Read Genesis 3.
2. Do you view work as a gift? Why or why not?
3. What do you find rewarding while working?

NOTES

1. Alex Taylor, "Still Smokin'," *Fortune*, June 26, 2006, p. 52.
2. Doug Sherman and William Hendricks, *Your Work Matters to God* (Colorado Springs: NavPress, 1987), p. 99.
3. Douglas J. Schuurman, *Vocation: Discerning Our Callings in Life* (Grand Rapids, MI: Eerdmans, 2004), p. 51.
4. Agnieszka Tennant, "More Than a Job—Why Dennis Bakke Thinks That Work Can Be Fun—for Everyone," *Christianity Today*, July 7, 2005, p. 35.

REASONS TO WORK

Everywhere across the grounds of our school, one sees JOY banners scattered across our buildings. The JOY banners stand for "Jesus, Others, Yourself." The hope is that our students, staff, and faculty will be continually reminded to live in such a manner as to place Jesus first, others second, and then oneself. The JOY concept is taken from Jesus' response in Matthew when asked which commandment was the greatest: "'Love the Lord your God with all your heart and with all your soul and with all your mind.' This is the first and greatest commandment. And the second is like it: 'Love your neighbor as yourself.' All the Law and the Prophets hang on these two commandments" (Matthew 22:37–40). The first summation encapsulates the first four commandments, discussing our relationship to God, while the second summation wraps up the last six commandments, discussing our relationship with others. Doug Sherman and William Hendricks, in *Your Work Matters to God*, suggest that all five reasons for work flow out of this verse: "Love God. Love others. Love yourself. In the broadest and simplest terms, this is what God wants done in the world."[1] My five reasons for work are adaptations of these authors' insights; mainly we work to serve, to satisfy, to supply, to send, and to sanctify.

Serve: We work to serve the needs of God's people. For most of my friends in the medical profession, it is quite easy to draw a distinct purpose for their work; simply put, they desire to heal people and as a result improve their quality of life. In education, teachers understand the importance of inspiring a child to a lifetime of learning. Likewise, the Lord sees the profound influence some teachers have on others because He attaches a warning, suggesting, "Not many of you should presume to be teachers, my brothers, because you know that we who teach will be judged more strictly" (James 3:1). In other professions it is more difficult to see at first glance how we serve others. For example, a MARTA (Metropolitan Atlanta Rapid Transit Authority) driver who drives the same trains back and forth each day may fail to see his usefulness; but thousands of people each day depend on MARTA for cheap, convenient, and punctual transportation to and from work in order to provide for their families. In the same way, the young man who loads crates of milk into trucks night after night in order to pay his way through college also serves others. That milk may provide nourishment for the next Martin Luther King Jr. However, not all professions providing a service fall under meeting the needs of God's people. For instance, a crack dealer or a developer of porn sites would clearly fall outside biblical boundaries. God's system of work is an elaborate system. Each of us has the opportunity to play a role in a much larger serving network.

Satisfy: We work to satisfy our own needs. The difference between needs and wants has become grayer as our society's materialism reaches a fever pitch. I admire those individuals who maintain a simple lifestyle. There's John whose wardrobe never increases. Whenever he receives or purchases a new pair of pants, he donates an old pair. There's Robert, a former colleague of mine, who takes public transportation to work (over an hour each way) in order to save money on gas and do his part to help the environment. Then there's my mother-in-law who has lovingly made everyone's lunch in her family for years in order to save money and to ensure a healthy meal. Unfortunately, for most of us, as our income increases, so do our needs. My first job was as an admissions counselor at Wake Forest University. Like most first jobs, the pay was relatively low because it was a transitory two-year position. After being promoted to assistant director of admissions, the very first thing I did was upgrade having professionally pressed shirts to a need. I'm half-ashamed to say I have not ironed my own shirts since 1997. The apostle Paul understood true contentment: "I am not saying this because I am in need, for I have learned to be content whatever the circumstances. I know what it is to be in need, and I know what it is to have plenty. I have learned the secret of being content in any and every situation, whether well fed or hungry, whether living in plenty or in want. I can do everything through him who gives me strength" (Philippians 4:11–13). Working helps provide for our needs. Staying rooted in Scripture helps maintain a biblical picture of properly determining the difference between needs and wants.

Supply: We work to supply needs for the ones we love. This particular justification for work is the easiest for most to understand, especially for the primary breadwinner in the family. How many times have you heard, "Who is the one who placed food on the table and a roof over your head?" Scripture is very clear on the subject: "If anyone does not provide for his relatives, and especially for his immediate family, he has denied the faith and is worse than an unbeliever" (1 Timothy 5:8). As with satisfying one's personal needs, the degree to which one must "provide" for one's family does vary. Too often I have seen fathers in particular use this as justification for working incessantly because they have mislabeled wants for needs. The recently purchased house far exceeds their needs as well as their budget. In order to compensate, the dad works extra hours to get additional money. Unfortunately for most, this obsession with working more is not a temporary situation. Living in debt becomes a lifestyle choice and dictates one's life. Steer clear of the old adage, "The rich rule over the poor, and the borrower is servant to the lender" (Proverbs 22:7).

Send: We work to send others. One of my greatest unexpected joys when I first joined the labor force was tithing. I love having money so I can give it away to help others in need, particularly those in ministry. "Each man should give what he has decided in his heart to give, not reluctantly or under compulsion, for God loves a cheerful giver" (2 Corinthians 9:7). Rick Warren, author of *The Purpose Driven Life*, has been so blessed financially that he and his wife have decided to shift to a reverse tithe, giving away 90 percent and living on 10 percent. Warren believes that "every time [he] give[s], it breaks the grip of materialism on [his] life."[2] How much joy must the Warren family receive from the millions of people their generosity affects!

My school offers a handful of mission trip opportunities over spring break. A component of the trip preparation urges the students to send support letters for their trips. Even though many of the students' families will pay for their trips, asking for monetary and prayer support includes others in the ministry. Our working helps send others. "He who has been stealing must steal no longer, but must work, doing something useful with his own hands, that he may have something to share with those in need" (Ephesians 4:28).

Sanctify: We work because we love God. God created man for work. For me, when I am not productive, I feel worthless. Last year our school hosted a Serve-His Day, a day during which our school sent our kids all over Atlanta to serve in various ministries. In order to get the kids thinking about Serve-His Day, Julie Pack, the coordinator, placed little hands and feet all over the school to remind the students that we should be the hands and feet of Christ. We are the ones whom God has chosen to perform His work. We have the privilege of seeing God's handiwork up close. God desires us to work, exhorting, "Whatever you do, work at it with all your heart, as working for the Lord, not for men" (Colossians 3:23). Working helps give purpose to our lives. "God invites us to have communion with him as co-workers while God brings the world to its consummation in the new heaven and new earth. Human work is a duty and a godlike activity."[3] Loving the Lord comes in many different shapes and sizes, as does how one loves neighbors and oneself. We are all part of a larger intricate system.

SEASONED ADVICE

Jill Jordan McMillan, sixty-five; professor emerita of communication, Wake Forest University, Winston-Salem, NC:

As a young person, I accepted the latent mythology that finding one's career was the single most important pursuit in life, and helping me do that was clearly the central goal of the educational institution at all levels. Slowly I came to realize that one's career is only a vehicle—albeit a significant one—for best pursuing one's spiritual education and journey. In short, what began to dawn was a profound insight from John Bradshaw (paraphrased)—we often mistake the life journey as a *human* endeavor, with a little spirituality thrown in for good measure (usually at 11 A.M. on Sunday morning), when it is, in fact, a *spiritual* journey, with just a bit of necessary humanness (i.e., a job, house, vehicle, paycheck, etc.). Blessed with the skills and intellect to choose several career paths—as were virtually all of my student advisees at Wake Forest—it was less important that I choose exactly the "right" career than that I understand my career as a means to an end, a venue to grow and mature spiritually.

This shift in focus is critical because it profoundly recasts the ups and downs of professional life:

> 1) It reframes professional setbacks and "disasters" as *opportunities* to learn something that good fortune might disallow.
>
> 2) It regards each person—even difficult coworkers, abusive bosses, and formidable adversaries—as our *teachers*, whose "piece of the truth" (Aristotle, *Nicomachean Ethics*) we need to be exposed to and to embrace.
>
> 3) It changes our measure of *success*. For example, money, possessions, and prestige may take backseats to loyalty, patience, kindness, humility, physical/psychological health and well-being, etc. Doing may be replaced by being, and the cultural icon of arriving might be surpassed by the enjoyment of the never-ending journey.
>
> 4) Finally, and most important, re-prioritizing the essential goal of life shifts the ultimate measure from one externally driven by social norms and convention to one that seeks to hear instead, "Well done, good and faithful servant."

I would never suggest that one's choice of a career and how it is conducted is unimportant because it might be just the arena for the greatest spiritual growth. (And do not be surprised if much of that growth is uncomfortable, no matter how prestigious and lucrative the job!) I would just have us remember the ultimate purpose of the career—to remind ourselves, as did Dan Milgram in *The Way of the Peaceful Warrior*, that even the mightiest spiritual teachers may come to us as gas station attendants . . . or carpenters.

POINTS TO PONDER

1. Which of these five reasons for work most resonates with your ideology?

2. Which reason for work is the hardest for you to accept?

3. What have you learned about yourself as you have joined the workforce?

NOTES

1. Doug Sherman and William Hendricks, *Your Work Matters to God* (Colorado Springs: NavPress, 1987), p. 88.
2. From a talk by Rick Warren, "Leadership Is Stewardship," Leadership Summit 2005, at Willow Creek Community Church, South Barrington, Illinois.
3. R. Paul Stevens, *The Other Six Days* (Grand Rapids, MI: Eerdmans, 1999), p. 123.

4

DISCERNING YOUR CALL

Come to a full realization of who you are and what you have been gifted to do, and embrace it eagerly. Do it. Be true to who you are. Be true to your call, true to how God has made you. Your call is not a superior call or a more sacred call; it is merely your call.[1]

As *American Idol* has shown the world, millions of people love to sing. These people drive all over the country in order to seize their opportunity to shine. Their passion and belief in their abilities drives them. In most cases, loved ones encourage them to audition by affirming their abilities. It never ceases to amaze me to see those blessed individuals who are tone-deaf, and yet their relatives croon their praises. During those auditions, Simon always seems to say what the majority of the world is too polite to say. Nevertheless, the majority of those who audition are denied the opportunity to compete. *American Idol* offers us a snapshot of how one discerns one's calling. Tim Keller, the lead pastor of Redeemer Presbyterian Church in New York City, suggests that the ingredients of calling are affinity, ability, and opportunity.[2]

We are all hardwired with special gifts and talents. These are the activities we enjoy doing—our affinities. For most of us our affinities emerge in our childhood. Think back to your days as a youngster. What activities did you enjoy the most? What hobbies could captivate your attention for hours? What did you dream about doing for the rest of your life? For me, like most kids, many occupations grabbed my attention for short periods of time, but one stood out among the rest. In fourth or fifth grade I decided I wanted to be an author and a cartoonist. I had always loved to draw and to doodle; so I began to write short stories and poems and to illustrate them. Most of my stories revolved around Sqwabbles—a crazy-looking group of creatures that were a mix between a frog and a football. I was heavily influenced by the Smurfs. I had many different types of those crazy little critters. My gifted teacher encouraged me to submit some of my stories to children's magazines, and when a few of them were published, this publicly affirmed my abilities and gave me opportunities to succeed. In addition, my mom's cousin was looking for a mascot for a new program at her school. She ended up paying me to create a Sqwabble specifically for her school.

I would do anything for money. When I was four years old, I went door-to-door selling my pictures for five to ten cents. Entrepreneurial blood ran through my body early in life. Needless to say, my mom made me give all the money back. I joined the Charles M. Schulz fan club and was pretty sure that I wanted to become a cartoonist. Schulz's impact on my life proved so profound that upon his death, I wrote to my local newspaper: "As a child, he inspired me to draw, be creative, and express myself through an unknown medium. Cartooning captured my spirit. . . . Though I no longer treasure my sketch pad, Schulz's lovable characters still remain etched on the backdrop of my mind."[3] Early in my life I found something I enjoyed doing, others affirmed my ability, and opportunities opened up because of my talent.

Middle school sent my plan into a tailspin when I had a

mediocre art teacher who failed to motivate me the way my grade school teachers had. At the end of the first semester, I changed my focus from art to drama. Looking back, it's amazing how huge an impact teachers had in my life. This realization eventually led me into education. The main reason I attempted drama was that my sixth grade teacher's assistant strongly encouraged me to audition in seventh grade because I was such a ham. I was hooked immediately. That spring I tried out for the musical and was awarded the lead in *The Coolest Cat in Town*. I know what you're probably thinking—is that Rogers & Hammerstein or Sondheim? Well, neither. It's a lesser known, extremely fun musical that never really caught on apparently. I loved the limelight. I loved everyone looking at me, and I loved the attention I received from females. I stopped writing and focused more on acting, singing, and athletics. My affinities had changed, probably in part because I received more affirmation for my acting abilities than I did for my cartoon creatures.

In college I was a business major and a theater minor. I was always told that your minor is where your heart is, while your major is where your head resides. I didn't really know what I wanted to do. Nothing stirred my heart. All of my friends seemed to have their careers figured out, but I honestly didn't have any idea. During my senior year I had the lead in *Big River* as Huck Finn. The musical is constructed in such a way that Huck serves as the narrator for the entire show. Thus I was on stage the entire performance, calling for six to nine hours of rehearsal every day. Applying for jobs that fall didn't really fit into my schedule. During that process I considered going to New York with some friends after graduating, but I kept coming back to, "Would I still enjoy acting if I were getting paid? Would the profession allow me to have a family?" In my heart, an acting profession wasn't as important to me as a profession that would allow me to invest in my family.

CALLING

During the winter of my senior year, for the first time I thought about education as a profession. The profession seemed to fit well with my ultimate goal of having a family as well as with my gifts and talents. I decided to pursue a job in admissions at my college in order to give me more transferable skills for secondary education. Ultimately, I believed my long-term goal was to achieve the position of principal or headmaster. I thought my equal passion for the arts and athletics would make me a more balanced administrator than some I had seen while working in admissions. Again, the opportunities presented themselves, so I seized the chance.

As I've grown older, I continue to realize that I have no idea where the Lord will lead me. I have interests and things I enjoy doing, my affinities, but the Lord has a mysterious way of orchestrating events that don't always make sense until you look back on your life. I've always lived my life with the belief that I can do anything upon which I set my mind, a thought that is noble but grossly inaccurate. If I am honest with myself and my abilities, the truth is, I cannot do absolutely anything I set my mind upon because we are all hard-wired with certain gifts and talents. Life is much easier running inside God's will than running outside of it. Choose a profession based on enjoyment rather than monetary compensation. Ultimately your passion will be rewarded—if not in this life, then in the next. I've noticed a shift in recent years—young professionals do not want to pay their dues in the workplace. I think there's a strong sense of entitlement among some people, an attitude that will close doors. In order to guard yourself against the predominant theme of entitlement, clothe yourself in humility. Don't be so concerned with finding the "perfect" job. Every job will teach you something about yourself. As a result, it is critical that you learn as much as you can from each job.

In each job I have acquired skills that have helped me in

some facet of another job. Invest in yourself. In our society, skill sets are more important than résumés. Take opportunities for growth over financial windfall opportunities. When you don't feel challenged or you find yourself complacent, it may be time to move on. If you are engaged or married, changing jobs is no longer an independent decision. Every person is different; don't try to place yourself in the typical model. As cliché as this sounds, follow your heart, but temper it with wisdom. Your heart may be telling you over and over to start your own business, but if you are never successful, then maybe you should do something a little less entrepreneurial. Trust your friends and family. "It is in community that we come to an appreciation of our gifts and abilities—by noting and having others note how we contribute to the well-being of the community. It is in community that we see how we are unique and how the desires of our hearts are different from but complementary to the desires of others."[4] Too often we miss this point. More than likely, if others do not affirm your giftedness in an area, maybe that pursuit/career/profession is not your calling.

Finally, God either opens the doors of opportunity or closes them. A good friend of mine, Will, has always been blessed with oratorical, musical, relational, and theological gifts. All of those close to him have always encouraged him to work in the ministry, either in music or from behind the pulpit. After college, Will bumped around in a variety of vocations. Nothing seemed to fit, and doors continued to close for one reason or another. Will's plan for his life did not match the Lord's, for "in his heart a man plans his course, but the LORD determines his steps" (Proverbs 16:9). Once Will was true to himself and listened to those affirming his gifts, doors of opportunity began to swing open for him. Regardless of how talented you may be or how much others affirm you, if the opportunities do not present themselves, at some point you must objectively ask, "Is this where the Lord wants me?" All of us need to discern for ourselves the fine line between perseverance and stubbornness. Are we trying to force our will, or is the Lord trying to teach us through our struggles and adversities?

SEASONED ADVICE

Stephen Arterburn, fifty-three; founder and chairman of New Life Ministries (www.newlife.com) and Woman of Faith Conferences; radio host and author of over sixty books; Laguna Beach, CA:

Problems led me to my current career path. I had a lot of problems in college. I really got lost in promiscuity. I had been a Christian for a long time, attended a Christian college, got a girl pregnant, paid for her abortion, and really hit rock bottom. I didn't really have any alternatives other than to go up because I was pretty far gone. At that point I rededicated my life to Christ and made a very dramatic change in my lifestyle. Most of my friends saw such dramatic changes, they questioned my sincerity. As I marched on to recovery, I found that others felt comfortable approaching me with their questions and problems. Seminary seemed the natural progression for me with a focus on counseling. I graduated with a degree in counseling and administration. My dream at the time was to run a counseling center at a college. I came to understand that there are individuals with severe difficulties whom the church has a hard time reaching or understanding, and I wanted to be part of something that would reach out to them and help them. Transformation stirred my soul. I thrived on helping people turn back from unhealthy life choices.

My biggest hurdle, though, early on in life was simply knowing what to do, knowing which direction to go. I remember I was offered a job as head of a health-care company, and I just didn't feel it was the right thing to do. My heart's desire was to have a career that served as the catalyst for transforming the lives of others, not merely a job for financial gain. Sometimes you have to walk away from great opportunities in order to do great things for the Lord. Shortly after turning down the job, in 1988 I started New Life Ministries, specializing in Christian psychiatric programs, and that has proven so fulfilling. Like all new businesses, it would have been extremely helpful to have degrees in accounting, law, public relations, and broadcast journalism. But the main thing I didn't know was to not be embarrassed to ask others with more wisdom how to do things, how to get things done. I had a lot of drive, determination, and commitment, but I didn't have a lot of insight into things. If I had just been willing to ask those with insight earlier in life, many obstacles would have been much easier. Anybody in his twenties or thirties should know that nearly everyone in their fifties is more than willing to tell others what they know or help them get a start in what they're doing. The best advice anyone ever gave me was to hire good people. Unfortunately, I was never very good at that; so I would hire good people the second time or the third time around. I've been blessed to have extremely strong people around me. Surrounding myself with good people allows me to create boundaries for my life. For instance, although I speak and travel a good bit, I limit my travel to two nights a week. As a result, I pass up many great opportunities, but my main priority is my family.

Goals have always been important in my life, but not as formally as others. I had a goal to write and speak, serving as a voice in the Christian community. One of the goals I had was to sell a million books. It would have been great if the first book sold one million books, but it took quite a few books to reach a million. A goal that turned into a ministry was my desire to encourage women. Eventually the desire sprang into Women of Faith conferences. Like all endeavors, we encountered challenges along the way, but we persevered. Our first conference was horrible, but we worked through all the challenges because we were going to do whatever it took to be successful. For those beginning their careers, their expectations are probably too high and their dreams are probably too low. You should dream big, plan big, but be willing to lower your expectations with the reality that you find. So many are never driven to act because they want it to be easy; they want to be a big shot, a big speaker, or a best-selling author, but they do not realize that most big-time personalities started small. All of us must pay our dues.

POINTS TO PONDER

1. Read Matthew 25:14–30.
2. With whom do you most identify? Why?
3. Make a list of all of your affinities, abilities, and opportunities.

NOTES

1. Gordon T. Smith, *Courage and Calling* (Downers Grove, IL: InterVarsity Press, 1999), p. 52.
2. See http://www.redeemer.com/learn/resources/keller_qa.html ("Work").
3. Tim Clodfelter, "Goodbye to the Gang," *Winston-Salem Journal*, January 2, 2000, Accent 1D.
4. Smith, *Courage and Calling*, p. 48.

5

WHERE DOES YOUR
TRUST RESIDE?

*If you know with certainty that God loves you and that He desires
good for you, what is there to fear? What is there to dread? What is
there to be depressed about? I am not making light of fears, doubts,
or depression. They are normal human responses. Hope, however,
compels you not to remain in a state of fear, doubt, or depression.
Hope encourages you to raise your eyes and look for the dawning
of a new day. Hope calls you to anticipate God's best.*

CHARLES STANLEY, *THE REASON FOR MY HOPE*[1]

When disappointments, difficulties, or defeats roll your way,
how do you respond? Where or in whom does your trust
reside? How do you know if you really heard *the call*? A few
years ago I heard a great story on this issue. The story begins
with a young inexperienced etymologist desiring to watch a butterfly emerge from its cocoon. So he waited and waited until one
morning the cocoon started to crack. Immediately this young
man's heart began to race, his eyes grew wide, and he braced
himself for this incredible event. Well, after an hour or so he realized this soon-to-be butterfly wasn't making a whole lot of progress; so he thought it would be a good idea to help the insect by
tearing the cocoon. Upon tearing the cocoon, he watched as the
insect plopped to the ground with dwarfed wings and a disfig-

ured body. The etymologist didn't realize that the insect required the struggle to become the beautiful creature God intended it to be. The struggle of freeing itself from the cocoon would enable the butterfly to learn perseverance, endurance, patience, and in the end fulfillment of the dream. This butterfly was denied the dream because he was not allowed to endure the struggle and learn from the process.

We are no different than the butterfly. Just because you are called in a certain arena does not mean the road will be easy. A few summers ago my senior-year college Bible study had our annual reunion at Charleston. We chose Charleston because one of our own, Joe Gibbes, was finally appointed to a position in a church after a long, arduous journey. Joe felt called to "full-time ministry" his freshman year of college as he was talking to a friend who was an atheist; while Joe shared his faith, he heard from the Lord in his heart that this is what God desired for him to do. Even though he struggled with many aspects of his family's mainline denomination, Joe felt like God was pushing him to be a light in this denomination from the inside. After graduating from college and working a season as a ski bum in Colorado, Joe moved back to the South to live closer to the woman who would eventually be his bride, Amy, and to join a local church in that denomination.

Joe began the process of becoming a minister, which included facing a parish discernment committee. The committee met with Joe for eight weeks and unanimously affirmed his call. Next Joe met with the bishop, who was historically liberal. At times the bishop's ideology placed him at odds with Joe's church. Despite their differences, Joe proceeded through the process to the mandatory psychological evaluation, during which he was diagnosed through the Rorschach Ink Blot test as mildly but chronically depressed. He was immediately turned down.

While waiting a year, Joe used the time to look at himself

introspectively as well as to ask his friends and family if they perceived him to be depressed. No one did. Even the counselor Joe had seen four times believed Joe was pigeonholed because he attended a conservative church. In the meantime, a new bishop took over for the state, and Joe again made his case. Both men were encouraged by the meeting, and the new bishop signed off for Joe to take the Rorschach test again. Unfortunately, the results did not differ. Again Joe was denied. The bishop provided him a glimmer of hope and suggested that if Joe sought extensive counseling, he might reconsider. Joe believed through his prayers that he was still called, and this time he was truly willing to do whatever he needed to do. The church as well as his family and friends still affirmed his call.

As before, Joe entered the nine-month weekly psychotherapy meetings with a chip on his shoulder. One day in the car, however, the Lord spoke through a song on the radio, essentially asking, "Who are you to question the path I have for you?" At that point Joe surrendered himself to the process and challenged himself to be more vulnerable. Through that vulnerability, the therapist was able to point out areas of weakness, mainly dark areas within Joe that he had tried to suppress. As Joe brought those dark areas into the light, the Lord healed him. In the end the therapist never believed he was depressed; rather, Joe had some areas of his life with which he was not comfortable.

Approved by the therapist, Joe returned to the bishop and then on to another committee who found that Joe's beliefs clashed with theirs both ideologically and theologically. They were very confused with Joe's language, such as "having a relationship with Jesus." Ultimately they recommended, for the third time, that Joe not be approved for ministry in their denomination. Each time Joe would pray, "Lord, if You do not want me to be ordained or if I have heard You incorrectly, lay that on my heart. Make me feel like I could do anything else and be happy, be satisfied." He states, "But I never felt it. My desire only increased, as well as my affirmation of God's call on my life." Joe's rector still affirmed his call. So he went to seminary where many others affirmed his call as well. Through contacts at seminary, doors opened in South Carolina, which eventually led to his placement in a great church near Charleston. Although he's only been there a few weeks, Joe offers, "I feel like I am doing what I am called to do: to preach, to organize ministries, to teach, and to equip the saints."

Was Joe trying to force his will? Or did the Lord need to teach Joe some things about himself through his struggles and adversities in order to make him more useful for his future ministries? Each person's journey will take different twists and turns. Knowing when to let go is a mysterious aspect to God's will that evades a clear description or five easy steps. In Joe's case, the Lord continually affirmed his call while denying opportunities. Joe had to journey through the darkness in order to more fully appreciate the warmth of the light. Identify your affinities. Listen to others and how they affirm you. Wait for the right opportunities. But always keep in mind that your journey is your own. God's plan for you is unlike anyone else's on the planet. Thus, ultimately the only foolproof way to discern your call is to continually listen to God's promptings in your heart. Had Joe listened to the "professionals" along the way, he would have given up a long time ago. The Lord will judge each of us according to our ability to fulfill the specific call He has given each of us.

SEASONED ADVICE

Josh McDowell, sixty-seven; international lecturer and bestselling author; www.josh.org; Plano, TX:

My career didn't happen overnight; it was more like osmosis. I think that's how it is with most people. There were many times in my life when I made decisions to do whatever Christ would have me do. In other words, I would go anywhere, be anyone, and do anything that He wanted me to do and be. As I continued in my journey of obedience, he would speak to me through situations. For example, early in my career I was speaking in a junior high school in La Mirada, California, and I found myself frozen as hundreds of students poured out of their classrooms. As clear as a bell as the students passed by me, I felt as if God was saying, "I've called you to reach young people; don't turn back." That was a crowning moment in my life, but honestly, it was never one thing. It just happened. I don't really know how I got to where I am. Early on, right when I desired to become a youth speaker in America, I was sent to Argentina by Campus Crusade because the work was not prospering very well. It was not my choice to go there, but it was my choice to be obedient to God's calling on my heart, and out of that experience sprung my worldwide ministry. The crowds continued to grow as I traveled from university to university. And then out of the blue Bill Bright called and asked me to return to America and serve as a speaker for the cause of Christ at universities here in America. He said, "I want you to confront the radicals in the name of Christ." Within two weeks my ministry just happened.

Little things led to other things. Next thing I knew I was writing books. My second book, *More Than a Carpenter*, was written in forty-eight hours and now has sold over twenty million copies. Books were followed by videos, television, radio, movies—it just happened. I'm glad I didn't know how my career would unfold because if I had, it would have taken the suspense out of it. I learned if you are not obedient in the small things, God will not entrust the big things to you. I was so obedient in the small things that I spent an entire summer cleaning the floors and toilets at Arrowhead Springs for the staff. And what blows my mind is that I did those tasks with joy. The next thing I knew, I was the premier speaker at universities in America.

CALLING

Why should God trust you with big things if He cannot trust you with small things? Always make sure that your heart is right, that it's His will and not your will that you desire; be obedient in the little things. Do not start out by saying, "I am going to be a great speaker or world-renowned physician." No; tell yourself, "I need to be obedient in the next hour, the next week, the next month." Let God expand your horizons if He so desires.

POINTS TO PONDER

1. Read James 1:12 and John 7:38.
2. Journal about someone you admire in regard to how he or she responds to adversity.
3. How do you respond to disappointments and adversity?

NOTES

1. Charles Stanley, *The Reason For My Hope* (Nashville: Thomas Nelson, 1997), pp. 18–19.

6

HEARING GOD'S VOICE?

We all want to be heard, don't we? Listening to others' needs shows them respect. When Krista and I were dating, I would grab on to her every uttered word and trap it in my sealed vault, hoping to find an opportunity to demonstrate my keen listening ability. I desired to show her how much I cared about her by actively listening. Like most men, though, once we got married, my listening abilities rapidly declined, which is tragic because "there is probably no greater service that we give one another than to listen. When we listen to others, we attend to them, honor them, accept them and respond to what matters most to them. Nothing so demonstrates that we love other people as does listening to them."[1] After a few months of looking foolish early in our marriage, I have slowly learned to appreciate the things Krista loves by learning more about them simply by listening to her. In the same way, God desires for us to listen to Him.

How many of us would love for God to tell us in an audible voice whom to marry, what job to take, where to move, or which church to attend? While writing these thoughts on paper, I received an e-mail from a friend, Ben Wilson, who was updating his contact information for me since he was moving. I replied, "Why Lexington?" As if on cue, Ben responded, "I got a very palpable call to be here from the Lord. All of the pieces to this huge puzzle came together: I'll be able to do clinic and hospital work, it's close to our families, the small town suits our ministry style, and its close proximity to Winston-Salem offers great contacts and fellowship. I can testify to God's amazing wisdom, power, and patience in all of this. Thanks for asking." When people say, "I heard the call," inevitably it reflects the message of this e-mail. God might not speak in an audible voice, but He may instead communicate through a series of pieces all coming together like a puzzle. Secretly, though, most of us long for God to speak in an audible voice. We argue, "If God would just speak to me, then I would know exactly what to do."

I know I have always been envious of those persons in the Bible to whom God spoke directly. Whenever I think of God's speaking in an audible voice, Moses and the burning bush cross my mind first. God gave Moses a clear, discernible call, and Moses responded, "Who am I, that I should go to Pharaoh and bring the Israelites out of Egypt?" (Exodus 3:11). God graciously responded with, "I will be with you. And this will be the sign to you that it is I who have sent you: When you have brought the people out of Egypt, you will worship God on this mountain" (v. 12). Despite God's clear call, Moses continued to question. Doubts permeated his presence. Many people long for a burning-bush experience, but here was Moses face-to-face with God, and *he still doubted* his Creator. Trusting in God's sovereignty for our lives, even with a burning bush, still requires faith and a journey into the unknown.

Later in the Old Testament God spoke again in an audible voice, this time to a little boy. In 1 Samuel 3 we read, "In those days the word of the LORD was rare; there were not many visions" (v. 1). It took Eli, the priest charged with Samuel's care, three times before he realized that the Lord was speaking to young Samuel while he slumbered. "Go and lie down, and if he calls you, say, 'Speak, LORD, for your servant is listening'" (v. 9). Up to this point "the word of the LORD had not yet been revealed" to Samuel (v. 7), but his obedience to the Lord was apparent from the first time he said, "Speak, for your servant is listening" (v. 10). Afterward the Lord told Samuel his plans for judgment for Eli's family.

Samuel did not want to share God's plan for Eli's family, but Eli urged Samuel, "'Do not hide it from me. May God deal with you, be it ever so severely, if you hide from me anything he told you.' So Samuel told him everything, hiding nothing from him. Then Eli said, 'He is the LORD; let him do what is good in his eyes'" (vv. 17–18). From the beginning, Samuel listened carefully to God's call, and it was apparent to all that "the LORD was with Samuel as he grew up, and he let none of his words fall to the ground" (v. 19). How often do we hear God's gentle nudges but choose to let His words fall to the ground? How often does God speak through others and we choose to let their words fall onto the ground? How often does God provide a lifeboat, but we prefer to wait for the helicopter? What's the difference between Moses and Samuel? God spoke directly to both of them, but Samuel's spirit was *submissive*. He was ready to do whatever God asked. In order to listen to God effectively, a per- son needs to be submissive. Too often Christians craft their own will and want God to merely offer His stamp of approval.

In addition, God speaks through *situations*. For example, one of my college suitemates, Adam Sellner, worked for a parachurch organization for many years. This ministry changed his life in high school, spurred him on in college, and enticed him to join the team after graduation. Adam's gifts matched well with the ministry, and he enjoyed an abundance of success in the beginning. But as the days passed and the days grew long, something changed. Even though he was pegged the heir-apparent to his region, Adam was not sure that position was where God wanted him. Like many in ministry, though, he felt a strong sense of duty to stay the course even though he felt God leading him away. Eventually the gap in his heart grew so large that he sought advice from a counselor. For the first time in his life he was given permission to leave that ministry when the counselor said, "It's okay to leave." The counselor released the shackles from Adam's feet.

Once Adam left the ministry, his next step was not clear. At first he sold cars but felt extremely guilty. Adam explains, "Certainly God would much rather have me on the front lines with lost souls than hawking cars! What have I done?" He was confused and as a result set up countless meetings and interviews in order to chart a new direction. Eventually his restlessness was quelled by landing an entry-level job with a big national home builder. Once again, though, after a little while the voice inside his head began to speak up: "This is what you get. You wanted to be in business, and you forced your way in. Now here you are typing memos and formatting spreadsheets when you used to be preaching the gospel and leading disciple-ship groups!" Nevertheless he continued to climb the ladder until he was a general contractor. Despite his success, he knew deep down that building homes was not what God designed him to do. Now the voice was even louder: "Adam, in your disobedience you have run away from a calling in which you were naturally gifted to a job in which you have no natural instincts and in which you have to fight just to stay afloat. What are you doing?"

At that time the Lord brought Adam to a place of content-ment regardless of his circumstances and seemingly directionless and unfulfilled vocational life. He was content to stay put until

God moved him. Soon afterward new exciting job opportunities came Adam's way that he thoroughly enjoys and in which he feels challenged. "These jobs were clear callings from the Lord because I didn't orchestrate them. My burning bush was that I wasn't looking for something, but it came my way anyway." God speaks through our situations. Adam's situations showed him many different fields that were not good fits for him. Be aware of how God may be leading you.

Finally, although I do not practice the discipline of *solitude* enough, God desires for us to retreat into Him. In today's wired culture, access to others is instantaneous. Unplugging from the world must be intentional. If we do not take time to reflect and be still, then it is much harder for us to hear God. I would also ask you to ask yourself, "What are you afraid of?" People who never stop scare me, even those who are running for the Lord. How does a person who never takes time to be still know if he or she is running in the right direction? Dallas Willard suggests that solitude has risks: "In solitude, we confront our own soul with its obscure forces and conflicts that escape our attention when we are interacting with others."[2]

I never enjoyed Boy Scouts very much, probably due to a handful of unpleasant experiences; so the thought of retreating into the wilderness for days does not appeal to me. But for many, camping or long hikes are easy ways to unplug. In a recent *Catalyst* podcast, Eugene Peterson, author of *The Message*, shared that treasured times for his family were their weekly hikes. Every week they would travel to nearby trails, hike in silence for three or four hours, have lunch, talk about what God was teaching them, and go back home. For me, I journal, write, pray, and run. I am still an extrovert, but as I grow older, I find I cherish the times when I can be still and see what God has to say. God speaks in many different ways. These days it is rare to hear God's audible voice as in Old Testament times; nevertheless God does speak if you are willing to take the time to listen.

SEASONED ADVICE

Max Lucado, fifty-two; pastor and best-selling author; San Antonio, TX:

May I describe how a purposeful pause pulled me out of a spiritual desert? I can't blame my drought on the church. Attendance was soaring, enthusiasm mounting. We had outgrown our building and set our eyes on new property. Everyone pulled together to raise money and make plans. After two years of prayer and plans, gauntlets and victories, we made the move. And it nearly did me in. I remember standing in the new building before our beaming congregation, thinking, *I should be thrilled.* Instead, I was hollow, robotic, and mechanical. A friend noticed. (Thank God for friends who do.) He convinced me to . . . clarify my sweet spot.

Under the tutelage of executive coach and organizational consultant Rick Wellock, I wrote out my S.T.O.R.Y. "Describe some occasions when you did something you love to do and did it well" was my assignment. I reviewed my life, listing events of interested satisfaction and success.

- As an elementary student, reading every biography in the school library.
- Delivering an election-winning speech to the high-school freshman class.
- Neglecting other homework so I could write and rewrite short stories for a literature course.
- Presenting my first Bible lesson. Stunned that the middle-schoolers listened.
- Developing a detailed procedure for sermon preparation.

I devoted an entire day to passion review. After the counselor studied my reflections, he asked, "What one word describes your sweet spot?"

"Message," I replied without hesitation. I realized I exist to reflect God through clear teaching and compelling stories. He then asked the question that undid me. "Does your calendar reflect your passion?" We reviewed the previous six months of meetings, fund-raising, and facility development. "Seems like you are sitting on a lot of planning committees," he observed.

"I assumed I should since I'm the minister."

"Tell me, what do you discuss in these meetings?"

"Paint color. Parking lot size. City building codes."

"Do you enjoy them?"

"Slightly more than open heart surgery."

"Does your S.T.O.R.Y. include any successfully supervised construction projects?"

"No."

"Do people ever turn to you for strategic-planning advice?"

"No."

"Then what makes you think you should be giving it now?"

My exhaustion made sudden sense. I was operating out of my weakness, doing the most what I do the worst! With lesson learned, I resigned from every committee and returned to study and writing. In short order, energy resurged, and passion rekindled. Renewal began when I paused on purpose.

(Reprinted by permission from *Cure for the Common Life*, Nashville: W Publishing, 2005. All rights reserved.)

POINTS TO PONDER

1. Are you more like Moses or Samuel? Why?

2. When have you felt God speaking to you?

3. What has God taught you about your calling through situations?

4. What routines in your life have you established to help facilitate listening to God?

NOTES

1. Gordon T. Smith, *Courage and Calling* (Downers Grove, IL: InterVarsity Press, 1999), p. 191.
2. Dallas Willard, *The Spirit of the Disciplines* (San Francisco: Harper San Francisco, 1991), p. 161.

7

BLOOM WHERE YOU ARE PLANTED

There's something about blooming trees in the spring that always offers hope and rebirth. My wife and I were over at a student's house recently, and her mother mentioned that when they landscaped their yard, they made sure all of the trees bloomed. Similarly, as fairly new homeowners, my wife and I continue to upgrade our landscaping as our finances allow. I am always amazed how much joy a nice yard offers me, but then again it runs in the family. When I was a child, people would often chastise my father because he was always working in the yard, or the "park" as he commonly referred to it.

In Georgia, the clay-laden soil oftentimes poses problems for proper growth; so in order to optimize plants' success, preparing the soil is very important. Whenever we plant anything, we rush over to Pike's Nursery and purchase deep rich soil as well as mushroom compost to stimulate growth. After working the new ingredients into the soil, we carefully place the bulb of the plant under the ground, cover it, and water it sufficiently, anxiously hoping for success for the plant in its new environment.

In the same way, God desires for you to bloom wherever you are planted. So often the younger generation attempts to climb the ladder without living on the rung they currently inhabit. Jim Elliot, the missionary who gave his life in order to witness to the Auca people, had a single-minded focus once God gave him clear leading. In his case, the "'leading' was to Ecuador, so every thought and action was bent in that direction. Jim practiced what he preached when he wrote in his diary: 'Wherever you are, *be all there*. Live to the hilt every situation you believe to be the will of God.'"[1] These words are easier to read than to digest. Scripture offers us an excellent example of a young man who deserved to be bitter and jaded about his situation, but instead chose to embrace each situation and make the best of it.

Like so many families, Joseph did not get along well with his brothers. His father "loved Joseph more than any of his other sons, because he had been born to him in his old age" (Genesis 37:3) as evidenced by his crafting an ornate robe for Joseph. It appears that Joseph let his status go to his head a little. Early in his life he brazenly told his brothers of his dream during which "my sheaf rose and stood upright, while your sheaves gathered around mine and bowed down to it" (v. 7). Needless to say, hugs all around were bypassed for nefarious plans born in the jail of jealousy. Eventually a window of opportunity emerged, his brothers seized it, and Joseph was sold to Potiphar, the captain of the guard in Egypt.

Over time it became evident to all that the Lord was with Joseph, and when his master saw that "the LORD gave him success in everything he did, Joseph found favor in his eyes and became his attendant. Potiphar put him in charge of his household, and he entrusted to his care everything he owned" (Genesis 39:3–4). Under Joseph's leadership, abundant success fell onto Potiphar as well as his household. Eventually Potiphar's wife took notice of this striking young Jewish lad in her house and attempted to seduce him. When the plan went awry, she cried wolf and sent Joseph to the big house, jail. But it did not really matter. God was still with him.

The warden warmed up to Joseph and "put Joseph in charge of all those held in the prison, and he was made responsible for all that was done there. The warden paid no attention to anything under Joseph's care, because the LORD was with Joseph and gave him success in whatever he did" (Genesis 39:22–23). While in prison, Joseph interpreted dreams for new friends and eventually for Pharaoh. The Lord continued to bless Joseph. After Joseph told Pharaoh of the approaching seven years of prosperity followed by seven years of famine, Pharaoh placed Joseph in charge of Egypt, saying, "I am Pharaoh, but without your word no one will lift hand or foot in all Egypt" (Genesis 41:44).

In each stage of his life, Joseph made the best of each situation, and the Lord blessed him. The earlier stages of his life prepared him for an incredible honor bestowed upon him—the ability to save lives. Later in Genesis, we read that Joseph finally revealed his true identity to his brothers. During an emotional interchange, he proclaimed, "Do not be distressed and do not be angry with yourselves for selling me here, because it was to save lives that God sent me ahead of you" (Genesis 45:5). God's plan is mysterious. The smaller assignments in life prepare us for larger ones. As a result, it is imperative that "Whatever your hand finds to do, do it with all your might, for in the grave, where you are going, there is neither working nor planning nor knowledge nor wisdom" (Ecclesiastes 9:10).

When I first started working in admissions at Wake Forest, one of my mentors, Nate French (he now has a Ph.D. and dreadlocks halfway down his back), enjoyed giving me all of the tasks he did not favor. He would add with a Cheshire cat grin, "Creel, I'm helping you. I'm preparing you for knowing every aspect of this profession." He was right. After about nine months another assistant director left for another job, and I was asked to fill that position because of my diligence, attention to detail, and perseverance in reading thousands of applications in a relatively short amount of time. In my short life I've noticed that perseverance can cover a multitude of ineptitudes. Millions of people have great ideas and should write books, but writing takes discipline and solitude, both of which at times are very difficult to achieve. Do the job that the Lord has given you today well. Others will notice when you are successful. Try not to be in such a rush to reach the next level; enjoy where God has placed you today.

SEASONED ADVICE

Louie Giglio, forty-eight; founder and director of Passion Conferences and Sixstepsrecords; Roswell, GA:

Interestingly, I didn't really begin my career, and I am still not sure if I have one. *Career*, to me, sounds like the determined path of one's life, a series of steps and decisions that lead to a chosen end. My life has looked a whole lot like mystery revealed, taking steps with God not knowing fully where they would lead, but being blown away in the end.

For Shelley and me, the first non-career decision was made while I was a grad student at Baylor University. She (my wife now and a student there at the time) and I had started a small campus Bible study without a name with the desire to see real Jesus-life come to a campus filled with religion. Some people in my life thought I was crazy—committing career suicide. Just when I was supposed to be leveraging the obvious communication gifts God had entrusted to me, I was huddling with a handful of college students for zero pay and no prestige. But I knew that was where the action was. I knew it was where God wanted me to be.

As it turns out, our ten years there saw that small band

of students grow into more than twelve hundred a week. And though I do understand the power of institutions, I believe God used our ministry to reshape the landscape of the campus during our time there. The lesson in it all is that what's important in life is to realize that life is made up of moments, not careers. I want to be faithful in the moment to hear God's voice and follow Him, whether doing so seems to add up to career success or not. Now, twenty-one years later, I'm at the center of a college movement called Passion that I couldn't have even imagined in those early Baylor days.

To the emerging generation I'd simply say, "Decompress." Lay down the pressure of trying to figure out how to make the right decision for a lifetime and make the decision that is best today. Understand that's different from saying, "Don't worry about how today impacts the rest of your life." Instead I'm saying make the decision that is right, right now. If you do, you will discover a lifetime of the cumulative effect of being where God wanted you to be each step of the way.

POINTS TO PONDER

1. Would you consider yourself content in your current position? Why or why not?

2. What aspects of your job breed discontentedness?

3. What do you think God is trying to teach you in your current situation?

RESOURCES

Neil Clark Warren, *Finding Contentment: When Momentary Happiness Just Isn't Enough* (Nashville: Thomas Nelson, 1997).

NOTES

1. Elisabeth Elliot, *Through Gates of Splendor* (Wheaton, IL: Tyndale House, 1981), p. 9.

8

THEY PAY ME FOR THIS?

After years of accumulating interest, I finally spent my honeymoon fund after marrying the love of my life. Everyone I spoke to encouraged me to take my wife someplace more exotic, extravagant, or remote than we would ever visit on a typical vacation. So we spent our honeymoon in Bora-Bora in an over-water bungalow. Many times throughout the week I would turn and gaze into my wife's eyes, tell her I love her, and encourage her to take everything in "because we ain't coming back." Needless to say, it was an incredibly memorable week. One of the highlights of our trip was the shark feeding tour. Both my wife and I assumed we would watch our guides throw bait into the water and watch the shark feed. Well, we began to realize this might not be the case as our guides asked us our shoe sizes and handed us snorkeling masks.

From the onset of the trip, we were struck by the joy that emanated from our guides. Every guide smiled from ear to ear, continually cracked jokes about us being the shark bait, and wanted me to take their picture with my wife (not quite as funny). Once we arrived at the dive site, the guides jumped in first and started feeding the sharks, but it was hard to see below the water's surface. Soon after, we were all encouraged to hop in the water and get a firsthand look at the blacktail sharks as well as a lemon shark swimming deeper below the surface.

My fearless wife was the first to slide into the water as well as the first to plop herself back onto the boat at the first shark sighting. After a while everyone's comfort level increased below the surface with the sharks. Our guides found it particularly amusing to throw bait near me in order to lure the sharks my way. As the sharks darted around me, our guides howled with laughter as I would flail about uncontrollably in the water. At another dive site, one of the guides kissed a stingray on the mouth. Throughout our three-hour journey, all of the guides took turns playing instruments and singing local songs. I was enthralled by the joy these men displayed doing what they loved. I asked them if they had ever left Bora-Bora. They laughed and said, "Why would we want to leave?"

Much like the dwarves in *Snow White*, our guides "whistled" while they worked because they enjoyed what they were doing. In harsh contrast, an alarming amount of people do not enjoy their jobs. Those who do "whistle" while they work stand out, don't they? I've found that many people even resent those who seem to love their jobs because they haven't experienced the same joy. The author of Ecclesiastes writes, "So I commend the enjoyment of life, because nothing is better for a man under the sun than to eat and drink and be glad. Then joy will accompany him in his work all the days of the life God has given him under the sun" (Ecclesiastes 8:15). So, what's the secret to enjoying one's job?

Would you still enjoy your job if they did not pay you? Pete Higgins, a legend in the Georgia high school swimming world who won thirty-three state titles, has stated many times, "I've never worked a day in my life." He is amazed that the nationally acclaimed Westminster school pays him to do what he loves—mainly, teaching kids how to swim and the transferable qualities associated with the sport. We all long for that sense of fulfillment in our careers. Much like Eric Liddell, the Olympian in *Chariots of Fire* who chose not to run on Sunday because of religious beliefs, we strive to "feel God's pleasure" in our endeavors. Liddell felt fulfilled because he was utilizing the gifts and talents God gave him. Os Guinness suggests, "The truth is not that God is finding us a place for our gifts but that God has created us and our gifts for a place of his choosing—and we will only be ourselves when we are finally there."[1]

A year ago I scheduled a meeting with my headmaster, Zach Young, to discuss my future. By nature I'm a somewhat restless person. At times it is very difficult for me to be content in my situation. As usual, he opened with, "What's on your mind?" I shared with him my doubts and concerns. As we began to talk, I felt as though I was in a doctor's office; pearls of wisdom dripped from his lips, one of which included the question of what brings me joy. He encouraged me to think back to my childhood and remember what brought me intense joy. Gordon Smith reinforces this notion by stating, "It is worth noting that we will only be effective in fulfilling our vocation if we joyfully do what we are called to do. Without joy we cannot be effective. It is therefore very important that we come to terms with what it is that gives us joy, even if it means that we will not have comforts or wealth, fame or power."[2]

A few weeks ago I had an encouraging conversation with Stephen Graves, an executive consultant. I was interviewing him for this book, and before he allowed me to ask him questions, he wanted to ask me questions. I shared with him my story for about twenty minutes or so, answering all of his questions along the way. He paused for a moment and said, "At your core you're an artist, aren't you?" For one brief passage of time I felt as though all the stars had aligned. "Yes, I am an artist." I love to create, whether by singing, acting, writing, drawing, building a swim team, designing a building—in other words, any opportunity where my imagination has free rein. Do you feel trapped in your job? Think back through your life. What brings you joy?

SEASONED ADVICE

Mark Price, forty-two; former NBA All-Star; Alpharetta, GA:

Ephesians 3:20–21 always comes to mind when I reflect back on my basketball career. It states, "Now to him who is able to do immeasurably more than all we ask or imagine, according to his power that is at work within us, to him be glory in the church and in Christ Jesus throughout all generations, for ever and ever! Amen." My dreams started out small. Like many young basketball players, I hoped I would be good enough to play for my high school basketball team. By the time I graduated high school, I was named the Oklahoma player of the year and tied my dad's scoring record at the state tournament. I never dreamed I would be as successful as my dad. Surprisingly, college success also followed as I played for the Yellow Jackets of Georgia Tech. By the time I graduated from Tech, I was named All-Conference three times and ended up as Tech's second-leading scorer of all time. Again, in my wildest dreams I would never have painted such a storied college career, but God is so faithful.

Eventually God blessed me with the ultimate dream of basketball players everywhere: a place in the NBA. Each step of the way, God opened doors for me that I never thought would be open to a kid from the small town of Enid, Oklahoma. Who would have ever thought an average-sized kid from a town of fifty thousand would be a four-time NBA All-Star who holds the career free-throw percentage record at 90.4 percent? Not me.

Dream big dreams. God desires to bless you more than you could ever dream, but He desires men and women of obedience first. In other words, to experience God's greatest blessings, we need to faithfully walk with Him. Trust me.

POINTS TO PONDER

1. Read Psalm 37:4 and Hebrews 13:17.
2. Take a minute to write down five things that you love to do. Why do you love these activities? Now write down ways in which you could activate these joys in a profession.

NOTES

1. Os Guinness, *The Call* (Nashville: Word, 1998), p. 47.
2. Gordon T. Smith, *Courage and Calling* (Downers Grove, IL: InterVarsity Press, 1999), p. 41.

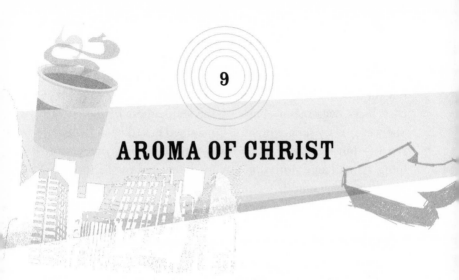

9

AROMA OF CHRIST

Every time I walked into the corner grocery store, I was amazed at the joy emanating from the grocery bag lady. She was a modest-looking woman but wore a smile that could convince Frosty the Snowman to roast marshmallows around an open fire. I was new to the area; so her smile was so inviting and comforting.

"Good afternoon, sir."

"Hello."

"Are you having a good day?"

"Yes, and you?"

"Oh, it's a beautiful day and a great day to be alive. Do you want these double-bagged?"

"No, I'm fine. Thank you."

There was nothing special about our conversation, but there was something different about this woman. Whenever I was in line, I felt encouraged. Apparently I was not the only one. Occasionally those in line would share fairly personal things with her. I was always shocked not only by how much they shared with her, but how much she seemed to genuinely care about the people whose groceries she was bagging.

CALLING

The years passed, and the depth of our conversations grew, but they were cut short by her heart attack. I, like many other customers, was taken aback by the suddenness of the events. She was not a young woman—I imagined her to be in her early sixties—but nevertheless she was missed. The grocery store hung a small sign notifying anyone interested of the time and place for the funeral. I don't really enjoy funerals, but I felt compelled to send my regards to this lovely elderly woman because I knew she did not have any family living and because I wanted to acknowledge the joy she brought me by simply smiling while bagging my groceries. Not surprisingly, I was not the only one who showed up to offer condolences. By the time I arrived, the parking lot was packed, and attendees were directing traffic to parking on the side roads. Hundreds, if not thousands, of people came out to honor the grocery bag lady. I had no idea this woman was so loved. Toward the conclusion of the tear-filled service, a friend of the deceased began to speak. "Most of you don't know this, but Dorothy loved everyone in this room. She was not the brightest woman or most talented, but as we all know, she was a very joyful woman. She never saw herself as a woman who only bagged groceries; rather, she claimed the six feet around her counter for Jesus Christ. You see, when each of you was in line, she would be praying over each one of you. The joy you saw in her face was Jesus shining through her."

This story affirms the notion that "the biblical approach to calling assures us that every believer is called into full-time ministry—there are no higher and lower forms of Christian discipleship."[1] Whatever God calls you to do—as a business person, a teacher, a sanitation worker, a doctor, a lawyer, a professional athlete, an entrepreneur—He desires for you to serve as a living testimony to His love and grace. God commands each of us to be the fragrance of Christ: "For we are to God the aroma of Christ among those who are being saved and those who are perishing. To the one we are the smell of death; to the other, the fragrance of life. And who is equal to such a task?"(2 Corinthians 2:15–16). A strong fragrance evokes memories, doesn't it? How many times does a certain perfume remind you of a loved one or the smell of a certain flower remind you of a simpler time?

According to an article in the *APA Monitor*, a publication of the American Psychological Association, "the connection between odor, memory and emotion has an anatomical basis."[2] In other words, certain odors are emotionally laden. God desires for us to be the aroma of Christ. He desires for His scent to linger long after we've left; He desires for His fragrance to pervade the air around us and envelop those who venture near us. Do you house the aroma of Christ?

You are God's ambassador in your sphere of influence. In the 1998 movie *The Mask of Zorro*, Anthony Hopkins (the retired Zorro) is training his successor, Antonio Banderas. When he's teaching Antonio swordsmanship, Hopkins begins in a very large circle, and as Banderas's skill increases, they move into a smaller circle and then finally into the smallest circle. The more skilled the swordsman, the better prepared he is to defend himself in a smaller setting. In the smallest circle, one is intimately acquainted with his surroundings, his senses are heightened, and he must be aware of every action within his sphere of influence. So it is with us.

Wherever God calls us, "all of our daily lives are woven together like a tapestry and presented as one whole offering to the Lord. In every activity of life we are to act as obedient partners of the Lord, giving those who live in darkness a taste of the holy God of truth, righteousness, and justice."[3] Do not compartmentalize your faith. In every aspect of your life, those who venture near you should be enveloped by the aroma of Christ.

This is no easy task, one with which I continually struggle. I hope someday to have a consistent fragrance like that of Dorothy, the grocery bag lady.

SEASONED ADVICE

Miriam Waggoner Heiskell, eighty-eight; director emeritus of The Heiskell School; www.heiskell.net; Atlanta:

In the fall of 1948 my husband was transferred to Coca-Cola's home office in Atlanta. At that time we had three children, ages five, three, and one. After only five days in Atlanta we learned that our eldest son, Andy, had contracted polio, which was a horrifying thing in those days. There was no serum, and not surprisingly, people were frightened to death of the illness. The first night after the diagnosis, the doctor told us Andy would more than likely not live through the night and that if he did live, he would probably never walk again. The doctor asked where my parents were. We called them in Knoxville and told them to come to Atlanta. American Airlines was gracious enough to hold an airplane for over forty minutes until my parents could get on board. When they arrived at Grady Hospital, we knelt down to pray. My father prayed because I was too emotionally upset to do even that. He asked God to spare Andy's life, and then he prayed, "Lord, we pray not our will, but that Your will be done. Lord, use this terrible experience to Your glory." The Heiskell School is the answer to that prayer.

Andy's life was spared that night. But the doctors said he would probably never walk or talk again for the rest of his life. Despite those discouraging words, we took Andy to Emory Hospital every day to go through intensive therapy through a program developed at Warm Springs, Georgia. Slowly Andy began to improve and recover. He began to walk and talk again. Then in May 1949 the doctors told us that Andy's recovery had been so miraculous that he would be able to attend first grade in the fall of 1949 as a six-year-old.

I had a background in early childhood education with one year's teaching experience, and I was concerned about Andy's ability to adapt to a normal school environment because he had been isolated from other children his age for more than eight months. So I invited fifteen neighborhood children to come to our house over the summer. I only asked that each of them commit to show up three days a week. My husband paneled our garage and built another room under our porch to give us two lovely rooms for our "school." After the summer went so well, the parents actually begged me to keep our little school open for their children and eventually their brothers and sisters. So I agreed to continue the school for one year, and then another year, and then another year.

This continued for several years until finally, at the end of about fifteen years, my husband said, "If you are going to do this for the rest of your life, then I want to build you a building." We were just a preschool for the first twenty-one years of our existence. Then in 1970 there was an educational crisis in the city, and the parents asked me to add a first grade. I decided to do it, even though it was in the middle of the school year, because there was a possibility that some of the public schools were going to close. We started with grades 1, 2, and 3 and then eventually added the rest. Parents and teachers worked day and night to make all of the necessary arrangements to accommodate more children. We saw the need and filled it. We even interviewed new teachers on the first big snow of the year! I didn't think any of them would show up, but they did, and we started school on schedule.

The Lord's hand has been on this school since its inception. The school belongs to the Lord; it's just been one small step after another. We did not plan to have a school; it was always the hand of God moving. It never crossed my mind to not do what He asked me to do. Today our independent, nondenominational, Christian school begins with two-year-olds and continues through the eighth grade. Our fundamental objective has always been that each child knows Jesus Christ as his or her personal Savior. Our teachers model their own faith in Jesus Christ in their daily interaction with the children entrusted to their care. Our building block and foundation has always been the Word of God, and it never occurred to me to do anything differently.

My aim in life has always been to glorify God and to fulfill the mission that God has for me. But when God provided an opportunity to impact children's lives through Christian education I found my life's calling. When I got married, my only career ambition was to raise a wonderful Christian family. Nothing else ever crossed my mind. Having a school was God's idea, and I just followed His lead.

What about Andy? He is currently executive vice president and investment manager of a large insurance company based in New York City. As he was growing up, there were some residual effects from his polio, but not enough to keep him from attending Atlanta's Westminster School in the early sixties where he ran cross-country and track. As Westminster's cross-country captain and top runner, he led his school to its first team state title and was its first individual state champion. He followed up his fall successes in the spring by becoming the school's first individual state champion in the mile. He then went to the University of Tennessee on a full track scholarship. The doctors said Andy would never walk or talk again, but God had a different plan, a plan to work a miracle in Andy's life. To God be the glory!

POINTS TO PONDER

1. What smells evoke strong memories for you?
2. Are there areas of your life you compartmentalize? If so what?
3. Like the two women in this chapter, what areas can you claim for Christ?

NOTES

1. R. Paul Stevens, *Playing Heaven: Rediscovering Our Purpose as Participants in the Mission of God* (Vancouver: College Publishing, 2006), p. 17.

2. *APA Monitor*, Vol. 29, No. 1, January 1998; http://www.apa.org/monitor/jan98/smell.html; accessed June 6, 2006.

3. Bradshaw Frey, William Ingram, Thomas E. McWhertor, and William David Romanowski, *All of Life Redeemed—Biblical Insight for Daily Obedience* (Jordan Station, Ontario, Canada: Paideia Press, 1983).

10

WHAT'S IN YOUR HAND?

A basketball in my hand is worth twenty dollars, but a basketball in Tim Duncan's hands is worth millions. A microphone in my hand is worth forty dollars, but in Katie Couric's hands it is worth millions. A paintbrush in my hand is worth a few dollars, but a paintbrush in Norman Rockwell's hand was priceless. What is in your hand?

I recently viewed a talk entitled *Leadership Is Stewardship* by Rick Warren at Leadership Summit 2005 at Willow Creek Community Church in South Barrington, Illinois. Warren began by retelling the story in Exodus when the Lord called Moses into full-time service: "Moses answered, 'What if they do not believe me or listen to me and say, "The LORD did not appear to you"?' Then the LORD said to him, 'What is that in your hand?' 'A staff,' he replied. The LORD said, 'Throw it on the ground.' Moses threw it on the ground and it became a snake, and he ran from it" (Exodus 4:1–3). Like so many of us, when God called, Moses had his doubts and fears. How could God use someone like him? What if those God intended Moses to lead wouldn't listen to him? What if he failed? Interestingly enough, the Lord's response was merely, "What is that in your hand?"

Warren points out that for a shepherd his staff represents his identity, income, and influence. And yet the Lord told Moses to "throw it on the ground." The Lord asked him to cast aside the object that embodied his hope and trust. In doing so, the Lord chose to transform his identity, his income, and his influence once Moses let go. It was as if the Lord said, "Let go and I will show you why you were really created."

God entrusts each of us with gifts and talents. Too often our hope rests in our ability to pull ourselves up by our own bootstraps. Freedom occurs when we realize we need to lay our gifts down so that God may work through us. In Moses' case, when he lay down his dead piece of wood, the Lord breathed life into it. After grabbing the tail of the snake, it immediately turned back into the dead piece of wood. A staff is merely a dead piece of wood unless the man holding the staff is willing to let it go and allow God to work through him.

There's a similar story in 1 Samuel about a young boy with a staff, David, whose brothers enlisted in Saul's army to combat the Philistines. One Philistine stood above the rest—Goliath. In fact, he was "over nine feet tall. He had a bronze helmet on his head and wore a coat of scale armor of bronze weighing five thousand shekels; on his legs he wore bronze greaves, and a bronze javelin was slung on his back. His spear shaft was like a weaver's rod, and its iron point weighed six hundred shekels" (1 Samuel 17:4–7). Each day the two armies would line up against each other, and Goliath would stand before the Israelite army and shout, "Am I not a Philistine, and are you not the servants of Saul? Choose a man and have him come down to me. If he is able to fight and kill me, we will become your subjects; but if I overcome him and kill him, you will become our subjects and serve us" (1 Samuel 17:8–9).

For many weeks no one would fight Goliath. King Saul failed to trust God to make good on His promise. As a result, his soldiers were demoralized and lacked the confidence to slay the giant. No one would step forward until David left his post shepherding his father's flocks to bring sustenance to his brothers. When David heard Goliath's request, he replied to those around him, "What will be done for the man who kills this Philistine and removes this disgrace from Israel? Who is this uncircumcised Philistine that he should defy the armies of the living God?" (1 Samuel 17:26).

David's discontentedness in the situation, his willingness to be used by God, and his faith in the living God propelled him to action. Not surprisingly many questioned his ability to bring down Goliath because of his youth, but David did not allow his youth to handcuff him since the Lord had given him previous victories over lions and bears while shepherding. After Saul reluctantly gave his approval, he clothed David in a large coat of armor with a large bronze helmet, but David replied, "I cannot go in these, because I am not used to them" (1 Samuel 17:39). Saul's trust rested in things of this world to bring David victory, but David cast the armor aside and trusted in God. He was confident that the Lord would bring him victory with only his shepherd's staff, five smooth stones, and his sling. And God did just that. In contrast, often I feel that I need to have everything in order before God can use me.

Do you see the trend here? Both Moses and David were willing to be used by God. Both men understood that their power did not come from what was in their hand but rather from what they were willing to set down. We all have gifts and talents that God wants us to use for His glory, but our trust cannot reside in the things of this world. Society beckons us to sing our own praises and announce our own worth, but regardless of what society might say, it's not about us. Only when these two shepherds set down their identities, their incomes, and their influences, and only then, were they useful to God. How does God desire to use you?

CALLING

Availability to God is the key to a successful career. Let me say that again: availability to God is the key to a successful career. The Holy Spirit is in our lives for many reasons, and one is guidance. A career occurs over a lifetime. Each of us will have many stops along a long journey. At each stop we need to learn all that the Lord desires us to learn and to stay when God calls us to stay and leave when he calls us to leave. Relax. God desires first and foremost that we love Him. I think too often I get wrapped up with always making the "right" move in my career. God will take care of the details if I am willing to set down my staff, set down my income, set down my identity, and set down my influence for His sake.

SEASONED ADVICE

Scott Reed, fifty-eight; retired chief financial officer of BB&T Corporation; Winston-Salem, North Carolina:

"Everyone thinks of changing the world, but no one thinks of changing himself"—a thought from Leo Tolstoy. I was no different when I began my banking career. I was wrongly focused on changing the world or at least *my* world. Fresh from MBA School, I wanted to take on the world of banking and become a man of substance and impact. I was self-centered! Like so many, I was seeking financial success, material gain, and titles. While I loved my Lord and needed Him as a constant in my life, the desire for "titles instead of testimonies" preoccupied me.

I had grown up being overly competitive in practically all that I did including academics and athletics as well as day-to-day relationships, wanting to be better than others. I had to prove I was not only acceptable and at least as capable as my peers, but superior. Oh, how I fought to be first accepted and then the best. Although I rarely was the best, certainly not in the classroom, I carried this competitive attitude on my shoulders with great pride.

So I entered the workplace with my sights set on worldly success. Having a sharpened, fierce sense of rivalry, I found that my competitiveness or sometimes combativeness would turn to envy and even jealousy in my relationships. I continually struggled to gain the upper hand, to be better than my friends and associates, to advance faster and further, to have the best. I could not be truly happy for someone else's successes and achievements. If others seemed to be getting ahead of me, my solution was to work harder and be smarter and sell myself any way I could. While I continued to progress at the bank and to receive financial rewards and titles, they were never enough. There were always endless mountains to climb and life obstacles to overcome. As one Christian leader says, "Selfishness turns life into a burden; unselfishness turns burdens into life." How true!

At this point in my life, God grabbed me and shook me hard when two of my three young daughters had separate accidents two days apart, resulting in head injuries that required neurosurgery. My wife and I were devastated and were quickly brought to our knees in prayer, asking God through Jesus to save our children. He did, and we began an intense period of being sanctified and dramatically growing in our Christian faith. As I studied the Word of God, I realized I wanted to be more like Moses and quite a bit less like Pharaoh. I decided that I wanted to seek testimonies, not more titles and material rewards. I desired, over time, to become others-centered as opposed to self-centered. I was tired of always competing and of the emotions that regularly produced in me. I wanted to truly glorify God in what I did and what He allowed me to achieve. I chose to focus more energy on relationships, caring, and sharing the gospel with others in my life.

I'm still working on this life change in myself, but I have come to understand that being a man means emphasizing relationships, having empathy and integrity, and living a life of service to others. This now includes short-term mission trips to

Russia teaching business concepts and sharing practical experiences with businessmen and businesswomen as well as, most importantly, opening my heart to them through my love of Jesus; loving and mentoring my grandchildren each day; and serving the Lord in Christian-based, nonprofit organizations. I pray that my steps backward in attaining this life focus will be followed by two steps forward.

The following are three other life lessons worth sharing. First, don't decide where you are going in life before you take an honest look at yourself and your God-given gifts, which we all have in abundance. You need to stop and fairly evaluate your strengths and weaknesses, skills and aptitudes, as well as what you enjoy most. After this evaluation bathed in prayer, the key is to establish the proper priorities for your life, both near-term and long-term, and then set out quietly and systematically to accomplish those priorities and fulfill your dreams. Obviously, I believe placing obedience to God and faith in His Son, Jesus Christ, to be first on the list.

Second, always have a positive attitude as the driving force in every area of your life. A positive attitude is not just a thought process but a discipline and a commitment. Colossians 3:23–24 says, "Whatever you do, work at it with all your heart, as working for the Lord, not for men, since you know that you will receive an inheritance from the Lord as a reward. It is the Lord Christ you are serving." Approach even the most minor task in this manner, especially at work when given an assignment by your boss. Each and every day you need to rededicate yourself to being positive—thinking positively and speaking positively. This is not something that can merely come and go; you have to work at it no matter what the circumstances. The winner is often not the most intelligent or the strongest, but the individual who adapts to the situation at hand and proceeds to make the most of it. Be positive. Remember for whom you toil.

Lastly, don't be afraid to fail. Failure is nothing but a means of learning, a means of growth. God uses life trials and tribulations and, yes, failures, to guide, teach, and shape us. I grew up afraid of criticism and failing, and looking back on my life I often want to cry over all my missed opportunities at school, in sports, and at BB&T. I did not want to risk failure; so I sat back and refused to even try. It has been said that the greatest hazard in life is to risk nothing. The person who risks nothing does nothing, has nothing, and accomplishes nothing. You may avoid embarrassment, suffering, and sorrow, but you cannot learn, feel, change, grow, or love. In a sense, only the person who takes risks is free. Be confident that you can make a difference. Remember, as is often said, "Even when you are falling on your face, you are still moving forward." The whole world is not against you—there are billions of people who don't care one way or the other. Life is either a daring, joyful adventure or a dull treadmill. Be a can-do, will-try person.

In looking back at my career, I see God's guiding hand at every turn, in every promotion that I received but did not always deserve or for which I was not the best candidate. God is so gracious and full of mercy. Purposefully set your expectations very high, reaching and stretching to become all that God intends for you to be. Focus on His program and being His man or woman. "And we know that in all things God works for the good of those who love him, who have been called according to his purpose" (Romans 8:28).

POINTS TO PONDER

1. What is in your hand that you are afraid to let go?
2. What is your greatest fear about setting down your staff?
3. Do you relate to Moses or David better in these two stories? Why?

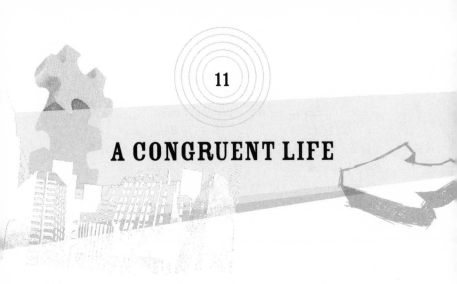

11

A CONGRUENT LIFE

Funerals remind me of my mortality. Unexpected deaths tend to sharpen my gaze on the most pertinent aspects of my life. At times life's details get lost in the ambiguous gray; yet, when God calls one of his saints home, it always gives me pause: "Would God be pleased with my life?" "Am I the man He hoped I would be?" "Do I take time out for those whom I love?" For some reason Harry Chapin's timeless classic "Cat's in the Cradle" echoes in my ears at funerals:

> And the cat's in the cradle and the silver spoon,
> Little boy blue and the man on the moon.
> "When you comin' home, dad?"
> "I don't know when, but we'll get together then.
> You know we'll have a good time then."

The song begins with a young boy desiring to spend time with his dad, but he's always too busy. The song shows the progression of the son's life as well as the dad's life. Toward the end of the song the tables have turned:

CALLING

I've long since retired and my son's moved away.
I called him up just the other day,
I said, "I'd like to see you if you don't mind."
He said, "I'd love to, dad, if I could find the time.
You see, my new job's a hassle, and the kid's got the flu,
But it's sure nice talking to you, dad.
It's been sure nice talking to you."
And as I hung up the phone, it occurred to me,
He'd grown up just like me.
My boy was just like me.

The words always penetrate my heart and convict me about honoring those I love and making sure I never take them for granted. As I observed everyone at one particular funeral, I started to reflect about the relationships of the deceased. Did this man's sons have time for him anymore? As a young man, did he have time for his sons? Did the family have any regrets?

On the altar stood two pictures—on the right, a happy man in a Georgia Bulldogs jacket and on the left a joyous grandfather with his four grandchildren sleeping on his belly. I did not know the man, but by the joy on his face and the heartfelt condolences offered, it was apparent that family came first, always. Pursuing the "perfect" job or sizable salary rings hollow against the grand scheme of things, doesn't it? We race, scratch, and climb to get to the top, but for what? Dying in your fifties always comes as a shock. While everyone was hugging and consoling each other, I felt a little out of place. So as usual I decided to seek those more on my level, the grandchildren. I found the four little rug rats running around smelling the flowers in the chapel and looking at the pictures. In between the two pictures was a brown box. Insert foot in mouth here.

"What's in the box?" I asked.

"Grandpa's ashes," replied the eldest grandchild.

"Grandpa was a big smoker," offered another grandchild, Matthew, who did not quite understand the situation.

How different are we from Matthew? How often do we not fully comprehend the reality of our situation? The infamous "they" suggest that the desires of our heart reside wherever our mind wanders. Where does your mind wander? If outsiders were to look pragmatically at your life, what would they see? What are the most important aspects of your life?

In the Gospel of Matthew, we find the familiar story of a rich young man who asked Jesus, "Teacher, what good thing must I do to get eternal life?" (Matthew 19:16). This question parallels many of us today. We desire the road map to the perfect life, asking, "What are the twenty steps to get there?" Raised in a society of instantaneous gratification, we want quick and easy results—why should the keys to unlocking eternal life be any different? We want the "good life" now. Jesus questioned why the young man was asking about what is good when "there is only One who is good. If you want to enter life, obey the commandments" (Matthew 19:17). From the text it is apparent that this young man was genuine in his desire to follow Christ. Jesus shared with him the commandments he needed to follow, and the young man naively said he had kept them. Earlier in the Sermon on the Mount, Christ explained that man lacks the ability to keep the commandments of his own volition. To not physically murder someone is not enough; rather, "anyone who is angry with his brother will be subject to judgment" (Matthew 5:22). To avoid physical adultery is not enough; rather, "anyone who looks at a woman lustfully has already committed adultery with her in his heart" (Matthew 5:28). God's standard for our lives far exceeds any standards we could set for ourselves.

After the young man said he had kept the commandments, Jesus told him, "If you want to be perfect, go, sell your possessions and give to the poor, and you will have treasure in heaven.

Then come, follow me" (Matthew 19:21). The young man "went away sad, because he had great wealth" (v. 22). The price proved too high; the cost was too much. Much like little Matthew who did not fully comprehend his grandfather's passing, or like the rich young ruler who was not willing to give up his most prized possession, what lack of congruencies reside in your life?

In contrast, Luke offers a wonderful story of a man desiring his outward actions to reflect the change within his heart. When Jesus entered Jericho (chapter 19), he encountered a wealthy tax collector named Zacchaeus. Historically, Jewish tax collectors were viewed as traitors to their people because they gouged their citizens for Rome's benefit. Not surprisingly, the crowd muttered when Jesus chose to have dinner with Zacchaeus. But Zacchaeus was so moved by Jesus that he said, "Look, Lord! Here and now I give half of my possessions to the poor, and if I have cheated anybody out of anything, I will pay back four times the amount" (v. 8). God desires this type of congruency in our lives.

About one month before I met my wife, I challenged my sophomore Bible study guys to write their obituaries as if they would die that day. Afterward we all shared our obituaries and asked each other if the obituaries were accurate. What areas in our lives did we need to improve in order to make these obituaries a reality? Were our lives congruent? Life moves very quickly.

As Christians it is critically important to take time to reflect on the whole of our lives. At your funeral what pictures would sit on your altar? Family? Friends? Money? A picture of your office building?

SEASONED ADVICE

Dr. Michael Youssef, fifty-seven; founding rector of the Church of the Apostles and the president and CEO of Leading the Way; Atlanta:

One of the problems of reflecting back is that most of us either see all of the positive or all of the negative. It is an arduous task to be honest and transparent and not become preachy in that task. As I reflect back on my twenties and thirties, I feel that I was living my life in a hurry. I did not take time to enjoy the journey. I wanted to get there the fastest way possible. I saw vacations with my family as something I needed to do—and not necessarily enjoy. Back then I could not wait to get back from vacation so I could go to work. Let me give you an example of what one five-year period of my life was like:

I was studying full time for my Ph.D.; working as the managing director of a worldwide ministry; traveling over a hundred thousand miles in overseas travel and twenty thousand miles of domestic travel; writing books; lecturing to world class leaders and preaching on every continent; teaching a weekly Bible class in Atlanta. And by the way, I was a husband and a father of three children.

In this type of active lifestyle, my relationship with God and what I did for God often got blurred and indistinguishable in my mind. The most important advice that I can give someone in their twenties and thirties is basically twofold and comes from my own failures, not my successes.

1. Be sure not to confuse activity for God with your walk with God.

When I found myself flat on my back for two weeks, not able to do any work for God, God began to teach me that He wants me, my time, and my focus before He wants what I can accomplish for Him. Ever since that time, I seldom schedule early morning appointments. The first two hours of the day belong to the Lord and no one else. I learned that unless and until I can minister to the Lord in worship and praise, I am not of much help in ministering to anyone else.

2. I wish someone would have taught me the vital impor-

tance of spending regular time alone with my wife, without the children.

I am grateful that back in 1982, before it was too late, my wife and I woke up to the importance of a weekly day together and a quarterly week together. That epiphany prepared us for the best years of our lives now as empty nesters. After thirty-five years of marriage, we are experiencing the best years yet.

It is my hope that this transparency will be an encouragement to someone.

SEASONED ADVICE

Joey Elwood, forty-one; president and cofounder of Gotee Records, Nashville:

There's so much I've learned over the last fourteen years as president of Gotee Records, but the biggest lesson I learned, I never really expected. All of the meetings, the successes, the failures, the hellos, the good-byes—all of it was not pointing to what I thought was the obvious—to make me a better record company executive. What I've come to realize is that all the experiences I've encountered in my job, while indeed it helped shape my professional career, were leading to the development of me as a husband and a father. It taught me to be more fearless, to seek to understand before I'm understood, and to not only meet conflict head-on but to work even more diligently to resolve conflict. And while all of that boded well for me as an executive, it factored so much more into my life as a leader of my home. In learning how to cover individuals inside the company, I learned what it meant to be covered by God and, again, what it meant for me to cover the most important thing over which God gave me domain—my family.

I'm very proud of all that has been accomplished by Gotee Records over the years, but I look back and realize that God was shaping me more as a man than as an executive. Whether it's triumph or disaster, you have to treat both experiences with the same wonderment: "What is God trying to reveal to me, and how does it apply to my highest callings in life?" Your finest moments in life will never be in the pursuit of your own destiny; rather, they will always reside in your humble quest to leave a legacy.

POINTS TO PONDER

1. Read 1 John 3:23–24.
2. Write your own obituary if you were to die today.
3. What areas in your life do you need to realign?

12

REWEAVING *SHALOM*

Growing up in St. Louis, I was blessed to have many Jewish friends. As a result of those relationships, I had a firsthand opportunity to learn about their customs/beliefs and to develop a sincere appreciation for their reverence for God. For instance, my cousin, Lauren, is Jewish. I remember the first handwritten letter I received from her when we were discussing faith matters; she wrote *G-d* instead of *God*. I questioned her about this spelling the next time I saw her. She said her omission of the *o* was a matter of reverence for God. Needless to say, the Jewish faith and culture have always intrigued me.

In Jewish culture, the term *shalom* is "used as a traditional Jewish greeting or farewell," but historically *shalom* is more often defined as peace.[1] The meaning of the word connotes a much deeper significance than this textbook definition. Rather, "the Hebrew word Shalom . . . in its fullness represented a vision of peace and spiritual well-being that was grounded in covenantal relationship with Yahweh and was reflected in all dimensions of life: economic, political, biological, and religious."[2] In other words, before the Fall God intended the world to exist as the perfect city. As Christians in a fallen world, we must align our lives with the Holy Spirit in order to craft a vision for the common good of all life. In addition, we must actively join in God's plan already in progress to reweave *shalom*.

God sent His son Jesus to show us the way and established the Church to be His hands and feet. Our first calling remains to be devoted disciples of Christ who continually work out our salvation in fear and trembling (Philippians 2:12). But we are also called to "establish justice, contribute to the common good and promote enjoyment of life in creation under God's reign. Particular 'callings' that cannot be used to serve this calling are not from God and must be forsaken. Christians should see all relational spheres of life as contributing somehow to God's shalom."[3] With this calling in mind, what does it mean to be countercultural for the common good?

A few months ago, I sat down with a lifelong mentor, Don Flow. He and his wife, Robbin, have been instrumental in my faith journey over the last ten years. Our conversations always spark my thinking and initiate change. This particular conversation occurred at a local restaurant after church. We sat for about two hours. Most of the interchange started with my asking a question and then furiously jotting down notes as I listened. Don first challenged me to explore the concept of *shalom*, which he defined as a flourishing city with five dimensions: goodness, beauty, truth, plenty, and order/justice.

These five dimensions encapsulate the five opportunities for us to live counterculturally for the common good. *Goodness* represents the social component of the flourishing city. Don said, "A market economy is a good thing, but a market society is not a good thing." Unfortunately, people are often viewed as individuals who do not possess inherent value. Recently Bono has led efforts to raise the awareness of those less fortunate in Africa; as a result, he was nominated for a Nobel Peace Prize. Bono's dedication stems from the belief that each person has value because we are all children of God by creation. People are not commodities. At Flow Motors, Don respects his employees as children of God. One tangible way he demonstrates his respect is his creation of an emergency fund for each of his dealerships. This fund is allocated by his employees to other employees whenever challenging situations arise. Typically one employee will share the obstacles of others, and then a cash gift is offered—no repayment accepted. Goodness reflects our desire to help our fellowman, and "the place God calls you to is the place where deep gladness and the world's deep hunger meet."[4]

In Genesis we read that God blessed Adam and charged him to "be fruitful and increase in number; fill the earth and subdue it. Rule over the fish of the sea and the birds of the air and over every living creature that moves on the ground" (Genesis 1:28). The second aspect of the flourishing city involves our charge to make this world aesthetically pleasing. As Christians, we are called to protect the planet in which we live and to remain good stewards of the resources the Lord provides. In addition, some in the world are called to *beautify* the world. My wife is an interior designer. Oftentimes her profession is difficult for her because she has difficulty finding purpose in it, but her job is critical to creating beautiful environments for others to enjoy. She creates order where there is disorder and frees others to pursue God's specific call for their lives.

The Gospel of John gives us Jesus' words, "Then you will know the *truth*, and the truth will set you free" (8:32, emphasis added). Flourishing cities recognize the importance of intellectual truths as well as the freedom they bring. Don is fortunate enough to lead a company of nine hundred employees. The majority of his workers are blue-collar workers, and some have trouble affording the rising costs of college. Don and his wife recognize the importance of education; so they started a foundation to help each of their workers' children attend college. Every employee is eligible to apply for a tax-free grant worth up to three thousand dollars each year for education. This example also dovetails into the fourth dimension: *economic*. Those individuals who have accrued wealth have a heightened responsibility to help others. A market economy is a good thing because it allows individuals to feel the tangible benefits of labor.

Finally, a flourishing city needs order and agencies to administer *justice*. Politically, our world needs men and women of faith to guide our nation. In a smaller microcosm of order, Flow Motors promises to fix your car right. If they misdiagnose a person's car, they'll fix it again for free. The undergirding principle is to honor their promises, and order is maintained when organizations keep their promises. If they do not keep their promises, there must be measures in place to administer justice.

God desires for us to help Him reweave *shalom* on this earth. We are all hardwired to help Him with His plan. He does not need us but hopes we will join in so we will be blessed by the experience. "Every genuine advance toward shalom is led by the Holy Spirit, who promiscuously chooses instruments of God's peace. In any case, Christian people seek the gift of discernment to know when and how to join existing movements toward shalom and where and how to start new ones."[5]

SEASONED ADVICE

Dr. Stephen Graves, fifty; Cornerstone Consulting and best-selling author; Fayetteville, AR:

I am frequently asked by men and women of faith in the workplace a revealing question. The setting and location may vary, but the question is constant: *"How can I approach my job with more kingdom intentionality?"* What follows are some of the distilled thoughts touching on that question.

Settle the concepts of workplace calling once and for all. God cares about your job, work and career. God calls people to a work station and work setting and it can change a number of times across your life. God brings purpose, energy and guidance to your daily work. God desires excellence on the job; this should be the norm, not an exception. God hopes you activate the Holy Spirit in your daily work.

Resolve your theology of influence and your approach toward "culture." This could be Christ *against* Culture—captured in the word *"withdraw,"* Christ *of* Culture—captured in the word *"acquiesce,"* Christ *above* Culture—captured in the word *"mandate"* or Christ *transformer* of Culture—captured in the word *"influence."* Activate a lifestyle belief in Christ the *transformer* of Culture—captured in the word *"influence."* Recognize the workplace as the landscape where salt and light can have their greatest impact. Engage in biblical learning around culture and influence. That could be achieved by studying the Scriptures, reading books, listening to sermons, interviewing experts or any other learning style that fits you.

Convert your existing work setting into a front-line, kingdom activity, base camp. Close the hypocrisy gap between being and doing. See the delivery of your skill set every day as the highest worship of your week. Sanctify the areas of money, time, relationships, attitudes, emotions, conversations, ambitions, reactions, decision making, etc. Clarify your particular style of covert/overt evangelism and messaging. Activate specific prayer for your work and the people in your work everyday. Evaluate whether you are "unequally yoked" with partners, work associates and other relationships. Discover your unique ministry signature. Embrace a "double bottom line" mindset regarding your work.

Identify your best 2-3 assets to "leverage" up into the king-dom. (Think Parable of the Talents.) Is it Money? Is it Time? Is it Strategic Thinking, Strategic Planning and/or Strategy Execution? Is it Relationships and Networking? Is it Encouragement? Is it Accountability? Is it Vision and Imagination? Is it Gray-Haired Experience?

Regularly evaluate the ROI (return on investment) of your kingdom investments and embrace an Acts 1 model to focus and scale your intentionality.

- Jerusalem—Your church/Your neighbors/Your co-workers
- Judea—Your larger community/Your region/Your industry
- Samaria—Your state, region or country/Cross culture
- Ends of the Earth—International environment/Cross culture

Invest in people first and ideas/causes second. Who has God put in front of you or for whom do you have a burden? Who has a unique voice/vision? Who has proven character and life skills? Who has early stage traction? Who has the possibility of multi-generational impact?

Root down in a healthy effective local church.

Don't be a church hopper. Don't be a self-serving consumer only focused on your needs. Don't sit safely in the stands. Put on a jersey and get engaged. Don't expect your church to fully understand and operationalize the work/faith integration. You might need to help lead this effort.

(Adapted from "Kingdom Agenda." Used by permission.)

POINTS TO PONDER

1. List personal examples of individuals reweaving *shalom*.

2. Where and how is God calling you to reweave *shalom*?

3. What component of the flourishing city is most difficult for you to grasp or put into practice? Why?

NOTES

1. See http://www.thefreedictionary.com/shalom.

2. Watson E. Mills, general editor, *Mercer Dictionary of the Bible* (Macon, GA: Mercer University Press, 1991), p. 664.

3. Douglas J. Schuurman, *Vocation: Discerning our Callings in Life* (Grand Rapids, MI: Eerdmans, 2004), p. 81.

4. Frederick Buechner, *Wishful Things: A Seeker's ABC* (San Francisco: Harper San Francisco, 1993), p. 119.

5. Cornelius Plantinga Jr., *Engaging God's World: A Christian Vision of Faith, Learning, and Living* (Grand Rapids, MI: Eerdmans, 2002), p. 118.

13

LEAVING THE HARBOR

God calls people. Whether it is the calling of Abraham to leave the land of Ur and go to places he did not know, or the calling of Moses, confronted with the burning bush; whether it is the calling of Isaiah, who encountered the glory of God, or the calling of Paul to bring the gospel to the Gentiles . . . an awareness of calling is both mysterious and powerful.[1]

Times of decision are never easy. Long gone are the days of our parents when one stayed with the same job for a lifetime. Most of us will not only change jobs but even careers, seven or eight times over our lifetimes. How do you know when is the right time to leave the harbor? Very rarely will the Lord provide you with a burning bush or a voice from above. Rather, after years of observation and experience, the common catalyst for change appears to be a *restless spirit*.

A few years ago my college roommate, Andrew Huck, sent a monthly report to friends and financial supporters entitled *Leaving the Harbor*. After college Andrew worked with Young Life in Knoxville, his hometown. To say that Huck, as he is affectionately known, was loved and revered is an understatement. Much like his mentor, Steve Chesney, Huck is a legend. In his letter, Huck recounts the gentle tugs on his heart that led him to embark in a new direction. He mentioned a profound encounter with a seminary professor who plainly asked Huck if he longed to be "a Christian Peter Pan for the rest of his life." There were also those times at night when he wrestled with the question, "Where do I see myself in ten years?" Numerous opportunities were placed before his feet, and yet none seemed to fit.

A mentor spoke simple words to him: "A man of God moves." A friend quoted Oswald Chambers: "You are not to spend all your time in the smooth waters just inside the harbor bar . . . you have to get out through the harbor bar into the great deeps of God . . . if you do not cut the moorings, God will have to break them by a storm and send you out."[2] And while perusing Knoxville bookstores he would inevitably be drawn to the "graduate school" section. One paragraph in his report encapsulates what so many of us feel in our hearts but are often afraid to verbalize:

> Dallas Willard says that the loneliest of moments is the time of *decision*. It is there that the weight of our future life clamps down on our hearts, that whatever comes will now be our responsibility. There are the second thoughts—and the third and fourth. Did I do the good and wise thing? Will others think I am a fool? What sort of path will this be? But in the midst of these anxious thoughts, there is forever a point of clarity. *When you hear the call, you must go.*

What does the call sound like? How can I be 100 percent sure this is God's will? I heard a wonderful sermon a few years ago during which the pastor suggested that no one will ever be 100 percent sure of the wisdom of decisions. Very good decisions may provide the decision-maker 80 to 90 percent clarity, but only hindsight offers complete clarity and confirmation as to whether we had made the right decision. Leaving the harbor proves dauntingly ominous because the unknown always invokes fear.

When we do hear the call, God still allows us the gift of choice. Well, kind of. Scripture offers a wonderful example in the story of Jonah. In the beginning of the book, the Lord spoke to Jonah: "Go to the great city of Nineveh and preach against it, because its wickedness has come up before me" (Jonah 1:2). Jonah, like many of his contemporaries, viewed the capital of Assyria, Nineveh, as a tyrannical empire. Why would the Lord call him to preach to a nation of Gentiles? Jonah chose instead to go thousands of miles in the other direction from Nineveh toward Tarshish. Most of us know what happened next. The seas grew rough, his crew members grew increasingly nervous, and in order to subdue the waters Jonah urged them to toss him into the sea, "and it will become calm. I know that it is my fault that this great storm has come upon you" (Jonah 1:12). The crew members wrestled with what to do because they did not want to die for taking a man's life, but eventually they relented and tossed Jonah into the water, where the Lord "provided a great fish to swallow Jonah, and Jonah was inside the fish three days and three nights" (Jonah 1:17). After lamenting his circumstances for three days, Jonah prayed to God from inside the fish. The last part of his prayer speaks to me a great deal: "Those who cling to worthless idols forfeit the grace that could be theirs. But I, with a song of thanksgiving, will sacrifice to you. What I have vowed I will make good. Salvation comes from the LORD" (Jonah 2:8–9). What idol is keeping you moored in the harbor?

For me, the answer is typically security and the trappings of comfort. My missionary friends, the Briggs, wrestled with the same issues before selling all of their worldly possessions and moving across the world to serve the Lord in South Africa. Each of them was a high-profile consultant living the yuppie's dream life, and yet the Lord called them, so they went. I admire each of them a great deal. After Jonah's prayer, God commanded the fish to expel Jonah onto dry land. Upon obeying the Lord this time and arriving at Nineveh, Jonah's words did not fall onto deaf ears. In fact, "when God saw what they [the Ninevites] did and how they turned from their evil ways, he had compassion and did not bring upon them the destruction he had threatened" (Jonah 3:10). The Lord used Jonah's act of obedience to spare "more than a hundred and twenty thousand people" (Jonah 4:11). To put it mildly, Jonah did not agree with the results; he thought the Lord should not spare the barbarians, and he grew very angry.

Like a splinter in your finger that never works itself all the way out, there are times in our lives when each of our spirits will become restless. On this side of eternity, all Christians will feel a certain sense of restlessness because this world as we know it is not our home; but vocationally, when we continually long for something more from our jobs, it is time to question. The difficulty lies in determining whether the Lord is truly calling you to leave your job or if you are just running away from a situation. The Lord uses challenging work situations to sanctify us. For example, generally speaking I have experienced minimal conflict with parents over the years, but occasionally the Lord uses parents to point out character flaws in me. Even though at first it stings, in the end if my spirit is contrite, those conversations help me specify areas for growth. Until we learn the lessons the Lord desires for us to learn, He will continue to place us in similar situations. A restless spirit is difficult to quench though. Assuming you are not running away from a challenging situation, if the Lord continues to provide a restless spirit within your soul, it may be time to start asking the Lord, "When and where to next?"

SEASONED ADVICE

Dr. Bill Satterwhite, forty-four; pediatrician; Winston-Salem, NC:

For most of my life, there have been few times when I have totally surrendered my will to God's will. In retrospect, I think I often "consulted" God about major decisions, but rarely did I totally lay my life at His feet and say, "Lord, I will do whatever You want me to do; I will go wherever You want me to go." The first time I think I truly submitted to the Lord occurred when I was in my late twenties when I was practicing law. As graduation from college approached, for many natural reasons I decided to go to law school. In the middle of law school, I wasn't sure if this was really for me, but I pressed on, finished law school, and got a job in a law firm. After about two years, I began to feel disenchanted, unfulfilled, and empty. I became very depressed. I was so low that I actually did pray and surrender totally to God, telling Him that I would go anywhere and do anything that He desired of me, but I wanted to do something that satisfied my soul, for practicing law was not "it."

I considered many different careers. I talked to many acquaintances in different fields. I got some career counseling. I prayed a great deal. A year later, I was in the hospital having surgery on my knee. As I lay there in the pre-op area, I had this overwhelming—mostly negative—thought: "I have missed the boat. Medicine is where I should be." My thoughts were more negative than positive because I was married with two small children, had a large mortgage, and had taken virtually no science classes as an undergraduate (unless, of course, you count Astronomy!). But I continued to pray about the idea of going to medical school. The cornerstone of my prayers was based around Proverbs 3:5–6, which says, "Trust in the LORD with all your heart and lean not on your own understanding. In all your ways acknowledge him, and he will make your paths straight."

CALLING

A pivotal moment came one weekend during the freshman-level Chemistry class that I had begun taking at night at a local university. My wife had gone out of town on a church retreat. I had the two kids by myself for the weekend. I had a test on Monday. I had found very little time to study during the weekend, and I was very tired from looking after the kids alone. I sat down at my desk to study, and I had so much trouble concentrating; I was exhausted. I began to pray. I said, "Lord, I can't do this. I am not a 'science guy.' I have a family. The path to becoming a physician is very long and very difficult. I want to trust in You, and I want to do whatever You want me to do, even if it is difficult. But I need a sign from You that this is the path You want me to be on. I need a strong, convincing sign, and I need it soon, or else I cannot continue down this path."

About two minutes later the phone rang. I said, "Hello." On the other end of the phone was a couple who knew me well. They said they had been praying for me and that they thought I would make a great doctor, and they wanted to help make that possible for me. They said that they wanted to give me $125,000 to attend medical school! (Private medical school tuition was about $17,000 per year then.) Needless to say, I was stunned. Surprisingly, I did not shout or turn cartwheels on the kitchen floor, as one might expect; actually, I was silent. I was silent because I knew that I was in the presence of the Lord. After thanking the couple profusely, I hung up the phone and said, "Okay, Lord. I will keep going down this path."

I totally submitted all subsequent decisions to Him. I prayed as I applied to medical schools at age thirty-one that He would make it clear to me where I should attend: I got accepted to only one medical school. I prayed about the curricula I should participate in (at the time this medical school had two different tracks): I got in perhaps the only one I could have passed as a lawyer-turned-medical-student. I prayed about what area of medicine I should enter: he closed the door into OB-GYN, which was originally top on my list, so I went into Pediatrics, and I am very grateful that I listened to Him. Through it all, I prayed that if the Lord suddenly wanted to turn me in a different direction, I would be obedient to Him again. There were many times the road was so difficult that I asked God, "Are You sure You don't want to send me down another path?"

Since that fateful moment when I received that phone call, I have tried to continue to submit all my decisions to Him. I have tried to teach my children (now I have four!) how to do the same thing. It is not easy. We all want to control our own destinies so much. The process of becoming more like Christ is not an easy one, and it is ordinarily a long one. Most characters in the Bible had to be shaped by God over many years before they were ready to be used by God for the tasks and purposes to which He had called them. So it is with us.

POINTS TO PONDER

1. Have you ever felt restless in your current job or vocation?
2. What is keeping you moored in the harbor?
3. Do you identify more with Jonah in the first part of the story or the second half? Why?

NOTES

1. Gordon T. Smith, *Courage and Calling* (Downers Grove, IL: InterVarsity Press, 1999), p. 9.
2. Oswald Chambers, *My Utmost for His Highest*, June 8; http://www.myutmost.org/06/0608.html; accessed July 23, 2007.

Part 2
CAREER

14

THE IMPORTANCE OF ENDURANCE

My sixth grade teacher, Mr. Cerutti, ingrained many wonderful truths in me, but none as significant as the importance of reading. In class each day before lunch he would sit on a rickety old stool and read a portion of William Goldman's classic fantasy, *The Princess Bride*. Every day we would revel in the details with each turn of the page. There are many wonderful nuggets to mine from this treasure, but one has stuck with me through the years: the importance of endurance. There's Princess Buttercup's enduring love for Westley, and Westley's enduring pursuit of those who captured Buttercup, but the most palpable example of endurance is displayed by Inigo Montoyo. As a small child, Inigo's father, a brilliant swordsmith, was killed by a man with six fingers on one hand who had commissioned his father to make a brilliant sword. However misguided his desire for revenge, Inigo dedicated his entire life to finding his father's murderer and one day standing before him to say, "Hello, my name is Inigo Montoya; you killed my father; prepare to die."[1]

After years of pursuit, Inigo finally found himself face-to-face with his opportunity only to be stabbed by his foil, Count Rugen. At first Count Rugen did not understand why this man was trying to kill him, but then the light dawned. "'You're that little Spanish brat I taught a lesson to," he said, coming closer, examining the scars. "It's simply incredible. Have you been chasing me all these years only to fail now? I think that's the worst thing I ever heard of; how marvelous."[2] Needless to say, Inigo slowly took the dagger out of his stomach, plunged his left hand into the wound, and kept going. He would not stop until he accomplished his goal. And he did.

We all have goals. We all have objectives set before us, some by chance and some by choice. Are you the type of person who makes excuses when unexpected hurdles block your path, or are you the type of person who leaps over the hurdles and keeps on going?

A colleague of mine, Jayne Burns, found herself in an overwhelming position when she learned that her breast cancer had returned after eight years. Unlike her first bout with cancer, she was facing metastatic, stage four breast cancer that had metastasized to both lungs and to the bones in her chest plate. According to her doctors, the diagnosis was terminal barring a miracle from God. Many tears were shed that first night as she and her three lovely daughters climbed into her bed, holding each other, crying deep sobs that only the threat of permanent loss can evoke. Her daughters pleaded with her to fight, but Jayne was tired, and she had lived much longer than anyone had ever expected. However, over time the heartfelt prayers of her daughters and the rallying support of the community instilled new hope in Jayne's heart. Honestly, I think most people believed Jayne's time was near, but Jayne fought.

Months passed with Jayne and loved ones fervently praying, Jayne improving her eating habits and tackling chemotherapy, and friends working to improve her living conditions. Her efforts proved miraculous when Jayne's next visit reported there were no cancer tumors anywhere in her body. The doctors were hesitant to share this miraculous news with Jayne, but eventually they acknowledged the fact that Jayne had experienced a medical miracle. The medical miracle offered Jayne a few more wonderful years with her family and loved ones. Unfortunately, cancer did return once again and despite Jayne's enduring spirit, she is finally at rest. She no longer needs to fight. The ultimate healer has granted her a healthy new body. Jayne's legacy for me will always be her enduring spirit and her willingness to fight regardless of what others thought. Challenges in the workplace cannot hold a candle to challenges we face in life and death situations, but every job does have a number of inherent challenges. The most "successful" people in the world are rarely the most talented but rather those with the most endurance.

The book of Nehemiah offers an excellent illustration of this biblical principle. Nehemiah found himself in a very reputable position as the cupbearer to the Persian king Artaxerxes. Nehemiah lacked power, but he had considerable influence and undisputed access to the king's ear. Burdened by the struggles of his people, Nehemiah requested permission to return to Jerusalem for a short while to help rebuild its wall and gates. Anticipating challenges, Nehemiah gathered letters from the king requesting safe conduct until he arrived in Judah as well as access to the king's forest for materials. After arriving in Jerusalem and appraising the situation for three days, Nehemiah "set out during the night with a few men. [He] had not told anyone what [his] God had put in [his] heart to do for Jerusalem" (Nehemiah 2:12). He sneaked out at night in order to inspect the walls of Jerusalem. Before sharing his God-inspired plan with others, Nehemiah did his homework. *A person of endurance anticipates and prepares for challenges along the way.*

One of Nehemiah's major challenges began with two local influential politicians, Sanballat and Tobiah, who "were very much disturbed that someone had come to promote the welfare of the Israelites" (Nehemiah 2:10). When these two learned that Nehemiah planned to rebuild the walls, each was incensed and insulted. So they "plotted together to come and fight against Jerusalem and stir up trouble against it" (Nehemiah 4:8). Learning of the attack, Nehemiah posted guards, gave an inspiring speech, and "from that day on, half of [his] men did the work, while the other half were equipped with spears, shields, bows and armor" (Nehemiah 4:16). In fact, many of the workers carried materials in one hand and swords in the other. Now that is determination.

Physical adversity was not the only challenge. Sanballat and his contemporaries also used psychological adversity, continually trying to ensnare Nehemiah by sending deceptive messages asking to meet under the umbrella of peace and harmony. After failing with the velvet fist approach, they turned to sending false reports, but Nehemiah would have none of it. Each time Nehemiah would go before the Lord in prayer, and the Lord would deliver him from their devilish schemes. *A person of endurance remains immovable by any form of adversity.*

Like most major projects, Nehemiah needed the help of countless others in order to achieve his goal. The third chapter of Nehemiah highlights the builders of the wall. Nehemiah skillfully encouraged all types of craftsmen and ordinary men and women to perform a litany of tasks with joy and harmony. Taking time to detail their contributions in chapter 3 cemented their place in history. At the completion of the wall in just fifty-two days (6:15), Nehemiah orchestrated a wonderful celebration with multiple choirs and a memorable worship service the likes of which Jerusalem had not seen for decades. *A person of endurance rewards and gives credit to those who give assistance along the way.*

If the book of Nehemiah were a movie, more than likely the credits would roll at the end of chapter 12 following the celebration, but Nehemiah finished the book with his return visit to Jerusalem. In returning to Jerusalem, Nehemiah found that Tobiah had defiled the house of God, the Levite portions had not been distributed, and the singers had returned to their fields (Nehemiah 13:6–11). Nevertheless, as any competent manager would do, Nehemiah tackled each challenge and made things right. He not only cared about the state of the wall but also about those people who helped him build the wall, saying, "Remember me for this, O my God, and do not blot out what I have so faithfully done for the house of my God and its services" (Nehemiah 13:14). *A person of endurance remains steadfast to the task's completion.*

SEASONED ADVICE

Tammy Trent, thirty-eight; singer/songwriter/author; www.tammy trent.com, Nashville:

As a child I loved entertaining people. I would do whatever I could to make people feel better or to simply put a smile on their faces. I come from a very musical family, so it seemed very natural for me to use music as my platform. I saw the effect music had on others' lives, and I wanted to utilize the gifts God gave me in a similar fashion. I knew that walking into the Christian music industry would be challenging both personally as well as professionally. Placing my personal life under a microscope would not be easy. Christian artists are expected to act a certain way, and rightfully so, but there is a strong sense of heightened responsibility attached to the industry. If you ask God for such a platform, you'd better be ready to step it up. I do my best to always be prepared whenever and wherever God calls, but we all fall short of God's glory. I've certainly made my share of mistakes, but I have always understood God's calling on my life and the responsibility attached to serving as a public figure.

Earlier on in my career my biggest challenge was simply getting my songs heard on the radio for the first time. I've always believed in working hard and running through any open door. So one sunny summer afternoon I hopped into my husband's Thunderbird super-coupe and drove around the country for two weeks, stopping at over fifty radio stations and twenty-five bookstores during that time to introduce myself to them, interview on the air live, and drop off free music for them to give away. I gave radio stations the opportunity to take me at my word and to get to know the real me, and that made all the difference in the world. Eleven years later, they know I was not a one-hit wonder; I'm still here today.

My goals changed after the tragic death of the love of my life, who died on September 11, 2001 while vacationing with me in Jamaica. He was free diving in The Blue Lagoon and never returned. Without question, his death and the surrounding circumstances have been the hardest thing I've ever had to face in my life. Just to keep living without the love of my life has been so challenging for me. I've learned that life can change at a moment's notice. Don't take anything for granted. Don't waste your time doing something you don't love doing. Life is a great adventure, so jump in with both feet. I have no idea what tomorrow will bring, but I'm not afraid of change. I'm ready for anything.

POINTS TO PONDER

1. What is the hardest task/goal you have ever tackled?
2. Why was it so difficult?
3. Read Nehemiah 5.
4. How did Nehemiah treat those who helped him?
5. What enduring challenge has God placed in your life today?

NOTES

1. William Goldman, *The Princess Bride* (New York: Ballantine Books, 1973), p. 275.
2. Ibid., p. 274.

15

THE IMPORTANCE OF CHARACTER

My Uncle Cork builds homes for a living. His real name is Cliff, but my grandma always had a thing for nicknames. My dad, nicknamed Jeep, is quite handy around the house. I am a good assistant; okay, I am an adequate assistant when called upon, but it's not something I truly enjoy doing. Before getting married, I had most major projects completed by my dad or a local handyman, Ernie. Ernie worked on homes for many years until he went into business for himself. The first time I met Ernie, he was wearing a white undershirt, cut-off jean shorts, a gold necklace, and a full-blown mullet. Needless to say, Ernie is his own man—the salt of the earth. He works hard for his living to provide for his family. In the time that I have known him, on two occasions he quoted me a lower price than he deserved. Halfway through both projects he ran into unpredicted snags that were completely out of his control. Both times he would say, "I like you, Colin, and I'm a man of my word."

Unfortunately, encountering men and women of character is no longer the norm. When a person of character crosses your path, he or she sticks out. Regardless of your profession, remaining a person of pristine character is of overriding importance. In 1 Samuel we see David's character tested time and again. After slaying Goliath, "whatever Saul sent him to do, David did it so successfully that Saul gave him a high rank in the army" (1 Samuel 18:5). Eventually, though, Saul's pride was supplanted by jealousy as the townspeople sang, "Saul has slain his thousands, and David his tens of thousands" (1 Samuel 18:7). From that time on Saul watched the favored son with an evil eye and concocted plan after plan to kill David. Saul's fear of David grew as it became more apparent that the Lord was with David, a fact evidenced by David's ability to overcome any obstacle placed before him. Eventually Saul's own son Jonathan pleaded with David to flee even though David asked truthfully, "What have I done? What is my crime? How have I wronged your father, that he is trying to take my life?" (1 Samuel 20:1). David fled, and Saul pursued him. Eventually Saul believed he had cornered David in the desert of En Gedi; so Saul took three thousand men to kill David.

Along the way, Saul needed to relieve himself; so he went into a nearby cave unattended. Little did he know that deep in that cave stood David and all his men. David's men proclaimed, "This is the day the LORD spoke of when he said to you, 'I will give your enemy into your hands for you to deal with as you wish'" (1 Samuel 24:4). Soon after, David silently crept up next to Saul and cut off a corner of his robe:

> *Afterward, David was conscience-stricken for having cut off a corner of his robe. He said to his men, "The LORD forbid that I should do such a thing to my master, the LORD's anointed, or lift my hand against him; for he is the anointed of the LORD." With these words David rebuked his men and did not allow them to attack Saul. And Saul left the cave and went his way. (1 Samuel 24:5–7)*

Why was David's conscience stricken? Shouldn't David have

been proud of himself for not killing his enemy when he was given a golden opportunity? David felt guilt for affronting Saul's dignity. Saul was God's appointed king; he deserved respect and allegiance. David displayed his respect for his king as he followed him out of the cave, addressed him as Lord, and bowed down to him. He then went on to reason with Saul—the same man who had been trying to kill him. When David completed his speech, Saul asked, "'Is that your voice, David my son?' And he wept aloud. 'You are more righteous than I,' he said. 'You have treated me well, but I have treated you badly'"(1 Samuel 24:16–17). Saul wielded a great deal of power, and he saw David as a threat to his power. But David remained true and faithful to his king despite the opposition. Even when given the opportunity to kill Saul, urged on to action by his fighting men, David chose not to believe that God's promise of deliverance meant killing Saul. David's character proved of greater worth.

Andy Stanley states:

> Your character is instrumental in establishing how long you will be able to hold on to the fortune afforded you by hard work and good luck. Your character is the internal script that will determine your response to failure, success, mistreatment, and pain. It reaches into every single facet of your life. It is more far-reaching than your talent, your education, your background, or your network of friends. Those things can open doors for you, but your character will determine what happens once you pass through those doors.[1]

In the working environment, your name is synonymous with your character. A colleague of mine who is working on an advanced degree in education told me, "In studying about administration, I realize at times I've been a real pain to my boss. I hate to think every time my name is uttered, my boss thinks 'Oh, the problem employee.'" The truth is, whenever your name is spoken, an immediate snapshot of you as an employee flashes before your boss. Your character serves as a window to what your snapshot will look like. Can you be trusted? Do you honor others with your words? Do you complain all the time? Do you make personal long-distance phone calls on your work phone? Are you happy? Are you, like David, willing to hold firm to your convictions even in the midst of great temptations, or are you like his servants who desired to travel the easy road? Good character takes years to craft and moments to destroy. So heed Socrates' advice:

> Regard your good name as the richest jewel you can possibly be possessed of—for credit is like fire; when once you have kindled it you may easily preserve it, but if you once extinguish it, you will find it an arduous task to rekindle it again. The way to gain a good reputation is to endeavor to be what you desire to appear.[2]

SEASONED ADVICE

Bob Worthington, fifty; CEO of SWH Properties, Dunwoody, GA:

Looking back, it is amazing to reflect upon how my priorities have changed since I began my professional life. The "shift" for me began at age thirty-four when my nine-month-old son tumbled down the stairs in a walker and broke his neck. This occurred at a time in my professional life when I was working seventy-hour weeks and was blinded by my ambition for rapid career growth and financial independence. I had become self-absorbed in a daily quest to advance *my* professional stature, to identify and land *my* next deal, and to receive *my* rewards. It all seemed appropriate. After all, my wife was home raising our three small children while I was working to lead us all to "the promised land."

While my son would eventually recover in full, there was a period of uncertainty that proved to be a wake-up call as I sought to make a deal with God for my son's healing. Basically I began to rethink the notion that I was in total control of my future and that career success and personal wealth were the keys to personal success and happiness. I began to focus on where I was, not just where I was going, and I began to focus on God and how my plan aligned with His.

I have come to realize over time that my success (and happiness) is measured less by how high I can climb, financially or otherwise, and more by how effective I am at lifting up others along the way. I find that individual accomplishment and high (even extraordinarily high) personal achievement ultimately prove to be insufficient and seldom endure with unhappy people. I also find that the happiest people I know live others-centered lives and through their focus on serving others have discovered the amazing rewards that are by-products of their giving. In short, truly happy people tend to be givers, while malcontents typically are takers. In today's climate of heightened materialism and the search for immediate gratification, realizing this earlier in the formative years of your career, rather than later, will better enable you to remain true and grounded. I would offer four suggestions:

- Recognize that in any chosen walk, your success will equate to your ability to truly distinguish yourself within the field. Success becomes highly improbable if your chosen profession was chosen for reasons other than sincere interest, passion, and a desire to achieve for the benefit of others. Do not become drawn to a career path simply because of where you perceive it has taken someone else. Rather, search for a heartfelt calling.
- Define a personal *core value system*, and *never* allow it to be compromised. A successful career, like a pyramid, is built block by block. Remember that any block that is obtained through compromise will become cancerous to your core values and your career foundation. It also can become habit-forming as you proceed to acquire the next block.
- Never value your accomplishment outside the home over your

responsibilities inside your home. In the end, this will produce a greater legacy and will have proven to be your life's most important work.

- Approach each day with an unbridled enthusiasm, optimistic outlook, and determined faith. It is always easier to identify where you want to go than it is to map a precise route for getting there. Successful individuals with an agenda of benefiting others possess an ability, through their positive attitude and unwavering faith, to regroup and push on rather than turning back when they encounter obstacles and resistance. Throughout the struggle they seem to enjoy the journey, grow in their self-confidence, recognize their self-worth, and ultimately find their way.

POINTS TO PONDER

1. Describe an instance or situation where you witnessed amazing character. What made it so amazing?
2. Read 1 Samuel 24. What do you notice about David's speech to Saul?
3. What areas of your character need work? Identify individuals whom you admire in your areas of weakness.

NOTES

1. Andy Stanley, *Louder than Words: The Power of Uncompromised Living* (Sisters, OR: Multnomah, 2004), p. 21.
2. See www.quotationspage.com/search.php3?Search=The+way+to+gain+a+good+reputation &startsearch=Search&Author=&C=mgm&C=motivate&C=classic&C=coles&C=poorc&C= lindsly; accessed June 29, 2006.

16

THE IMPORTANCE OF INTEGRITY

One spring evening a few years ago I was having dinner with a student, Tommy Binion—an engaging conversationalist, disarmingly genuine, incredibly affable, profoundly insightful, and passionate about learning. I cherish the time we spend together. In life there are times you connect with people for a variety of reasons, and Tommy is one of those students with whom I connected immediately when he helped me and a colleague start a Bible study for his class four years ago. Over the years the study has grown to include nearly half of the boys in his class. At dinner one evening, he gave me one of the best compliments I've received in recent years. We were discussing a commitment we had both made and how it was somewhat inconvenient, but I boiled it down to "I told Steven I would be there, so I need to go." Tommy responded with, "Through all the years of knowing you, letting your yes be yes and your no be no has left the greatest impression on me. It's a great quality." Earlier that week another teacher had mentioned to Tommy that it is not so much the biblical teachings in the study that will be remembered; the relationships formed in the group will be most cherished.

CAREER

A while ago, after an exhaustive search, my school hired a highly touted football coach from a nationally recognized program. His résumé oozed with accomplishments most football coaches would love to emulate. In addition to accolades from his playing days and his sterling coaching résumé, he also served in the ministry. This young man, a gifted orator and seasoned athlete, was expected to lead our school to a similar level of excellence in the game of football as well as to shape the moral fiber of the next generation of leaders. He verbally committed for five years. Initially I felt bad for this young man. Only in his late twenties, he was resented by many because of his youth and his catapulted success.

He started in late spring to prepare for the upcoming season. Immediately he met with his players and boldly proclaimed his goal to beat the top teams in Georgia and to secure a state championship before the freshman class reached graduation. His favorite saying was, "Work hard for me, and I'll work hard for you." The kids believed him. He changed our offense to a run and gun, fast, high-scoring offense and pampered the receivers in practice. Needless to say, they loved it. The results were instantaneous. Our first-year senior quarterback threw for over three thousand yards, placing him in the top tier of quarterbacks in the state of Georgia. In the midst of such success, however, there were signs early on that gave me pause, like our new coach's propensity to run up the score and continue to throw Hail Mary passes even when the game was easily in hand.

A few months later during the Christmas holiday, my wife and I were walking through a bookstore when a good friend and football coach, Jason Couch, shared the news that this new coach had resigned midway through his first year to return to his old school as an assistant coach, breaking his contract and breaking his word to a hundred young men who believed in him. Needless to say, I was shocked—not at his departure per se, but rather at his legacy of unfulfilled commitments. This coach also taught Old Testament to our students; he preached to them about the importance of covenants. His actions ruined our administrators' holidays, increased colleagues' course loads (including mine), left his co-Bible study leader in a lurch, and most importantly, his resignation shattered the young men he left behind. The betrayal these young men feel is palpable; to this day, they still choose not to utter this coach's name. Recently, at our yearbook dedication, a picture of our former coach appeared during a slide show, and joyous laughter was supplanted with a raucous array of boos. At our school his name fails to live up to the adage that "a good name is better than fine perfume" (Ecclesiastes 7:1). What amazes me most about the situation is that even now this young man fails to see the error in his actions. "Above all, my brothers, do not swear—not by heaven or by earth or by anything else. Let your 'Yes' be yes, and your 'No,' no, or you will be condemned" (James 5:12).

Integrity in all aspects of your life, whether in your personal or professional life, is monumentally important. Your actions are not performed in a vacuum. All of your choices or failures to fulfill your commitments will affect others' lives. Too often in our self-absorbed society we fail to recognize the complexity of the intricate web of consequences surrounding each of our decisions. Our AWOL coach left a mess for others to clean up; a person of integrity stands accountable for his or her actions. A person of integrity thinks through his choices and how those choices will affect those around him. A person of integrity does the right thing even at personal cost. Ultimately, "the man of integrity walks securely, but he who takes crooked paths will be found out" (Proverbs 10:9). My initial emotions of frustration were quickly displaced by waves of thankfulness—thankful that our coach's immaturity had been revealed and that his influence over our students was shattered. One can teach skill, but it is immeasurably more difficult to teach integrity. I would always choose a person of impeccable integrity over a person with a flashy veneer. In the long run a person with faulty integrity will cost your organization far more than dollars and cents.

SEASONED ADVICE

Studie Young, fifty-three; residential real estate agent with Harry Norman Realtors for twenty-five years, top producer city-wide, Atlanta:

There are so many times I think of my father's motto: "just do the right thing." It was his way of describing a life of integrity. I see it so often in my business. When making the sale is more important than actually helping the client with the best advice, the long-term results are really a diminishing return. It may not be a character trait that can be taught; it is an instinct, the gift of the Holy Spirit. I have been blessed by seeing my work as a ministry.

A few months ago I had a call from a person I had never met or even remembered. It seemed that I had given advice over the phone ten years prior about the value of a home to this stranger moving to Atlanta. She and her husband now wanted to buy a home I was familiar with and wanted my advice. When that stranger called me back, I asked her how she got my name. She reminded me that I had helped her ten years prior but at the time could not act. Ten years later I actually sold her a new home and sold her existing home and made a great new friend in the process.

Another example of my work as a ministry is unfolding currently: Zach and I have lifelong friends who are going through a personal trauma. The husband has been diagnosed with early Alzheimer's disease at the age of fifty-six—too young. This is causing a huge financial burden, and the couple must sell their home. Even though they live in another state, I am able to give advice about selling their home and help them make some decisions. In a time of stress and uncertainty, they trust my advice. It is a gift I can give.

Over the years as I have seen God at work in my work, I see how He has put people in my life for wonderful reasons. A ways back I knew it was time to get involved with a Bible study. I called eight clients whom I wanted to see more regularly. As a result we have been studying the Bible together for the last three years. Looking back I know that my relationships with my clients are based on trust. Our long-term relationships that remain well after the sale would not be long-lasting if there was ever a question that I would "just do the right thing."

POINTS TO PONDER

1. "Integrity in all things precedes all else. The open demonstration of integrity is essential; followers must be wholeheartedly convinced of their leaders' integrity. For leaders, who live a public life, perceptions become a fact of life. Leaders understand the profound difference between gestures and commitment. It's just impossible to be a closet leader."[1] When have you experienced duplicity in someone you admire?

2. Read Job 2:1–10.

3. How did Job react to his wife?

NOTES

1. Max DePree, *Leadership Jazz* (New York: Doubleday, 1992), p. 10.

17

THE IMPORTANCE OF FRUGALITY

One of the many benefits of working in education comes during the summer months. Many in education work during the summer in order to supplement their income. One recent summer I chose not to coach in order to write more and watch hours of mind-numbing television. After my daily dose of *ESPN*, I changed the channel and watched a special on "Leaving the Nest" on one of the early-morning shows. The interviewee talked about how as much as 40 percent of the college graduating class planned on living with their parents the next year because of credit card debt, student loans, and high rental prices. The truth is, a large percentage of the workforce walks into their first job with mountains of debt. Some of the debt is understandable, but much of it is avoidable. Often college students will choose their first job based on financial need and not necessarily because it is their heart's desire.

The hardest conversation my friend, Sandy French, had with her husband of ten years occurred the first time they sat down to write out their family budget. Three weeks before Sandy graduated from graduate school, she chose to take out a five-thousand-dollar student loan to help subsidize her fall trip to Europe. Over the next few months, she fell in love with a good friend of mine, procured a thirty-thousand-dollar-a-year job, and lived with her parents in order to save money for the wedding, but somehow she still spent nearly all of the five thousand dollars by the fall. By this time her father had already bailed her out three times by paying off her rising credit card bills. Sandy loved living. One of her favorite indulgences was attending concerts. After viewing over two hundred concerts, the debt continued to rise. In 1996 Sandy married Hunter with twelve thousand dollars in debt, her "negative dowry."

Hunter always planned on attending seminary. They attended an informational meeting at Fort Worth Seminary where the presenter encouraged prospects to get their finances in order before applying because most students coming in with over five thousand dollars in debt had a difficult time finishing. Sandy's tears were only overpowered by the subsequent guilt she felt from keeping her husband from following his dream. Hunter and Sandy moved back home to Maryland and constructed a stringent budget in order to free themselves from debt. When they were in the black, they would go to seminary. Honestly, Sandy really did not want to move to Texas, so she was pleased with deferring the move for three years, or so she thought.

Initially there was a great deal of pain in bringing their financial life under God's control, specifically for Sandy. Sandy parallels her financial picture to a big house where God owns everything but the closet. For her, the closet represented her sinful heart and the desire for no accountability in this area of her life. The stringent budget called the couple to live off of Hunter's salary and to use Sandy's to pay off the debt. *Financial discipline brings financial freedom.* Within six weeks of Hunter's new job with Verizon, they gave him a six-thousand-dollar raise because he was doing such a great job. In December he received another large raise and another in March, followed by a ten-thousand-dollar bonus in May. By July, Hunter and Sandy were packing their bags for Texas. Truly this is a story of God's blessing and God's grace.

Oftentimes one's lifestyle handcuffs a person to an unfulfilling job for fear of losing that lifestyle, or in the Frenches' case, because they had to make as much money as they could to pay off their debt. Do not let disobedience in your finances keep you from pursuing God's call for your life.

Obtaining a healthy view of money is not easy. But Scripture gives us clear teachings about it: "Whoever loves money never has money enough; whoever loves wealth is never satisfied with his income. This too is meaningless. As goods increase, so do those who consume them. And what benefit are they to the owner except to feast his eyes on them?" (Ecclesiastes 5:10–11). It is vitally important to *live below your means*. Our society is debt-laden due to individuals who are unable to determine the difference between needs and wants. Sandy never thought twice about charging concert tickets because she misconstrued a want for a need.

Living below your means includes, first, knowing the difference between a need and a want and, second, prioritizing the wants that are important to you. If attending concerts is important, great, but it may mean sacrificing in other areas. Christians need "to be content with a standard of living which is moderate, based mainly on necessities of life. On the other hand, Scripture does not outlaw the rich nor make it a sin to acquire wealth. God approves hard work and wealth is often the fruit of it. But the rich are not exempt from the call to all Christians to be moderate in their lifestyle, and to give sacrificially to the poor."[1]

Most of our ideas about money stem from our families. What are the good things your parents modeled as well as those areas you would like to change? Sandy never learned the value of a dollar until much later in life. I still remember when my dad took me to Federal Savings and Loan in Chesterfield, Missouri to open my savings account. My little blue book helped me understand the simple principle of interest at an early age. Even today my dad will still send me finance articles that he finds interesting. Many great books help parents teach their kids about money— for example, *Raising Money-Smart Kids* by Judy and Ron Blue. *Financial discipline brings financial freedom.*

After getting married, I created a budget for the first time. In speaking with my parents, I learned that they have never had a concrete budget. They have always been extremely frugal and responsible with finances, but my wife and I found that we needed a tangible way to keep track of our finances. The Frenches' budget tracked their finances down to the last penny using such programs as Quicken or Money. If you do not have a budget, one of the first areas to get squeezed out when money runs tight is your tithe, your giving to God. Scripture commands us to "honor the LORD with your wealth, with the firstfruits of all your crops" (Proverbs 3:9). An excellent way to ensure offering your tithe each month is to establish a separate account and have at least 10 percent automatically withdrawn from your paycheck each month. At the end of the year your tithe account should equal zero (except for the required minimum balance, of course). Timothy Keller suggests, "Be sure that your giving cuts into your own lifestyle so that some of the burden of the needy falls on you. Then, look at your own family's gifts and ministry opportunities and find the calling God has for you. Every person and family must minister in mercy."[2]

Krista and I made a budget not only because we desire financial freedom but also the freedom to do whatever the Lord calls us to do. Money is not evil, but the love of money is evil. Rick Warren, the author of the best-selling book *The Purpose*

Driven Life, experienced a tremendous windfall of financial prosperity. He and his wife made a conscious effort to maintain the same lifestyle and to implement a reverse tithe, living off 10 percent and giving away 90 percent. As a result of their financial discipline, countless lives have been changed out of their generosity. *Financial discipline brings financial freedom, which enables you to have a clearer picture of God's call for your life.*

SEASONED ADVICE

Zanese Duncan, fifty-five; consulting actuary and in leadership for several Atlanta parachurch ministries; Norcross, GA:

The Bible talks about money and possessions more than it does any other topic—in over two thousand verses. In Proverbs 13:7 Solomon, the richest man as well as the wisest man of that day, tells us that one can be rich but have nothing or poor and possess great riches. Although I have a background as a financial advisor to CFOs of governmental agencies and corporations in the area of public and private retirement plans, I need to be constantly reminded to saturate myself in biblical wisdom such as Solomon's regarding my own personal finances.

My parents and parents-in-law spent their formative years during the Great Depression. Their example in being wise with little rubbed off on my husband and me when early in our marriage we vowed never to charge more on credit cards than we could pay off completely once the bills arrived. When our children were born, we decided that rather than one parent working lots of hours, we both would continue working, but much fewer hours. Fortunately, we both had flexible schedules that permitted us to be involved in their lives. We had reduced income, but our church financial commitment was always a priority as well as saving for future college expenses. Our daughter's decision to leave public school to attend a private Christian school caused an unexpected depletion in our education fund. We continued to marvel at God's faithfulness in allowing her older brother to receive academic and other scholarships that almost completely covered his college expenses, effectively using *his* college fund for her private school expenses.

A few years later, separate company mergers caused my husband and me to be unemployed simultaneously, something we would not have chosen. Nonetheless, these events proved again that, as Psalm 24 indicates, the earth is the Lord's and everything in it and that, as Paul suggests, we would have sufficiency in all things and for every good work. Again God's abundant provision in several months of severance pay, rest, and trust allowed the two of us some time for other opportunities, including considerable volunteering at our daughter's high school in her final two years.

Paul tells Timothy in the end of chapter 6 of his first letter that we are not to trust in uncertain riches but in the God who gives us all things richly, that we should be rich in good works and ready to give and share (vv. 17–18). Only a few weeks into my time of severance from employment, an opportunity to begin a Bible class in the local public high school became available, something for which I had prayed for over ten years. My freed-up time allowed me to get in on the ground floor in helping set up that Released Time Bible option, off campus and for credit during the school day. God truly allowed me to be a part of something more than I could ever have asked or imagined (Ephesians 3:20), to see the fruit of those prayers in an amazing way.

King David reminds us as 1 Chronicles closes that everything in heaven and earth is the Lord's and that all wealth and honor come from the Lord. I personally know that God wants to bless us, and if we bless Him in return by being wise stewards of what

He has given us, He will bless us with wealth in many ways other than what the world knows as riches.

POINTS TO PONDER

1. Create a workable budget. Use this free online resource as a guide: http://www.free-financial-advice.net/budget.xls.

2. How did your parents shape your view of money?

3. If finances were not an issue, what career would you pursue?

RESOURCES

1. Howard Dayton, *Your Money Counts: The Biblical Guide to Earning, Spending, Saving, Investing, Giving, and Getting Out of Debt* (Wheaton, IL: Tyndale House, 1997).

2. A good financial web site about beating debt and building wealth is: www.daveramsey.com.

3. Ron Blue's Christian Financial Professionals Network helps you find a professional with a biblical viewpoint; www.cfpn.org.

NOTES

1. Timothy J. Keller, *Ministries of Mercy* (Phillipsburg, NJ: P&R, 1997), pp. 77–78.

2. Ibid., p. 78.

18

THE IMPORTANCE OF MENTORING

One of my greatest unexpected joys in education has been the privilege of coaching, mainly cross-country and swimming. During my last year coaching cross-country, the team was all huddled in a hotel room the night before the state championship. Each of the coaches sat in silence, choking back the tears as runner after runner thanked us for pushing them beyond what they thought they could handle, but more importantly, for continually encouraging them. Even as I reflect on that evening, tears well up in my eyes. How wonderful it is to have people who believe in you. Another example transpired last year at our swimming awards night. A graduating senior, Alex Bufton, had taken the time to compile a wonderful memory book that I will always treasure filled with pictures and letters from the team. All of the letters spoke to me, but a particular one from a graduating senior spurs me on when I question whether or not I am truly making a difference. He wrote:

> I want you to know that you mean an indescribable amount to me. Everything you say to me means so much, and I am incredibly thankful for you. I can remember you actually believing in me

when I was younger, and when we would talk about certain times and races you would get all excited with high expectations of me, maybe winning a gold medal or something. You always wanted something big out of me. When I was a freshman and sophomore, I can remember finishing a race and maybe not doing the best—but doing *my* best—and you coming up to me and saying, "you're getting there" and what you were really saying was, you're getting closer and closer to becoming what I want and believe you can be. You seemed to have a plan for me, an expectation of greatness. If I was there for the day we made our goal sheets, my number one goal would have been to make all your expectations come true and to not let you down. You cared and believed in me so much that I didn't want you to do all of that for nothing. Even though I didn't always do what I knew you wanted me to do and I didn't always make the smartest choices, believe me when I say afterwards I kicked myself because I knew exactly what you were going to say when you were going to yell at me. I knew that I was letting you down when you were the only one to stick up for me. You have made me the man I am today; you have been such an influence not just on my swimming but also on my entire character because you believed in me when everyone else saw a kid who just screwed up all the time. I would like to say thank you, Mr. Creel. Thank you so much for every second of time you have spent even thinking about me because you have no idea how much I appreciate it and how much I love you for every bit of it.

Love,

Stephen Durham

What an honor it is to be used by God. Everyone needs a cheerleader. Everyone needs someone who sees past all of the rough edges and simply says, "I know you can do it. I believe in you." Mentors are able to encourage others because they first felt the benefit of encouragement from others who believed in them. The ultimate encouragement comes from Christ. In Philippians Paul says "In all my prayers for all of you, I always pray with joy because of your partnership in the gospel from the first day until now, being confident of this, that he who began a good work in you will carry it on to completion until the day of Christ Jesus" (1:4–6). Mentors often serve as the conduit for Christ to carry others toward completion. Like so many areas of our lives, "the mentors we choose shape the person we are and the leadership we offer."[1] What makes a good mentor? This list is not all-inclusive, but it is a good start to a better understanding of mentoring.

Mentors have a vision for you. Like a historian at an antique sale, mentors see gold where others see junk. In seventh grade, at the urging of a former teacher, I auditioned for the fall play. I made the cast but soon thereafter decided to quit the play for some inconsequential reason. Thankfully, the director, Ms. Hart, gave me another shot when auditioning for the spring musical, *The Coolest Cat in Town.* Before she cast me as the lead, we had a heart-to-heart talk. She had a vision for me and was willing to give me another chance. My middle school drama experiences still remain some of my fondest because of one woman who never let me settle for anything less than what she knew I was capable of giving her.

In the same way, toward the end of his life Moses cast a vision for Joshua. Moses told all of Israel he was too old to lead them any longer and he would not cross the River Jordan with them, but Joshua would be his successor. Then, in front of all of Israel, Moses blessed Joshua with these words:

> *Be strong and courageous, for you must go with this people into the land that the L*ORD *swore to their forefathers to give them, and you must divide it among them as their inheritance. The* L*ORD himself goes before you and will be with you; he will never leave you nor forsake you. Do not be afraid; do not be discouraged. (Deuteronomy 31:7–8)*

Mentors have benchmarks for success. As my body begins to break down, I find myself with our school athletic trainer, Steve

Stepp, more often than I care to admit. While waiting for my treatment, I am always amazed at the young men and women who diligently rehabilitate surgically repaired joints for months. Inevitably a patient pushes further than he should in hopes of getting back onto the field. Steve reinforces, "Be patient. Stick to the plan." Successful rehabilitation is a delicate balance of time, rest, exercise, carefully setting benchmarks for success, and dialoguing about the results. As the patient reaches those benchmarks of mobility and strength, new challenges emerge, but only when the patient is successfully hitting those benchmarks repeatedly. In the same way that Steve measures his patients' progress, mentors use benchmarks to measure their mentees' progress. Those who are faithful in the small things will be faithful in the big things. Success breeds success.

Mentors display vulnerability. For many years while living in Winston-Salem, many wonderful families opened their homes, but more importantly their lives, to me. Each family taught me incredibly valuable life lessons by allowing me to see their families with their guards down, without the sheen of Christian prosperity. Oftentimes Christians feel an overwhelming need to create a facade of imperviousness to life's trials. In reality, our trials and our vulnerabilities enable others to recognize they do not have to be perfect. In the fall of 2006 a prominent pastor stepped down for personal reasons. Unfortunately, the consequences of his actions affected him, a congregation of thousands of people, but most directly his family. Both he and his wife composed statements to be read on their behalf during church; both individuals displayed immense vulnerability.

His wife's letter particularly struck me. She said that she loves her husband and is committed to him until death. Then she shared herself with the women of the church, saying, "For those of you who have been concerned that my marriage was so perfect I could not possibly relate to the women who are facing great difficulties, know that this will never again be the case. My test has begun; watch me. I will try to prove myself faithful." Wow. What a woman. In the face of adversity, this woman shines very brightly. She is an enduring example of a woman willing to be vulnerable for the benefit of others.

Mentors provide opportunities. We all need individuals in our lives to create opportunities for us or to keep us in mind when opportunities unfold. In junior high I started attending a youth group that had a profound impact on my spiritual development. The youth group was not that large, and as a result the parents and students worked hand-in-hand in order to orchestrate fun events and engaging programming throughout the year. At a very early age I was given a fairly significant opportunity by the Hunters, Dukes, and Vroomans to help shape and lead a group of people. Good mentors provide opportunities. While living in Winston-Salem, countless families pushed and encouraged me, but two families, the Barclays and the Flows, continually provided growth opportunities for me. At a challenging time in my life, the Barclays helped me stop thinking so much about myself and gave me the wonderful opportunity to train Young Life leaders by heading up the Quest program. In the same way, in the fall of 1999 the Flows sponsored me to attend the Foundation Leadership Conference in Tucson, Arizona as one of the next generation of leaders.

Despite the exhaustive expense, by sponsoring me the Flows were endorsing me. They were putting their necks on the line for me, saying, "We believe in this young man." Although no longer around, the Foundation was an intimate gathering (only a few hundred) devised with the hope of bringing together Christians who were at the top of their fields. For an extended weekend, I interacted with Christian business icons and sat at the feet of such great teachers as Ravi Zacharias, Joni Eareckson Tada, John Ortberg, Henry Cloud, Les and Leslie Parrott, Ken Boa,

Robert Wolgemuth, and the late Mike Yaconelli, just to name a few. What an opportunity!

Mentors model. Outside of Jesus, one of the greatest mentors of all time would have to be the apostle Paul. He served as God's conduit for birthing countless churches and disciples. In nearly every adventure Paul had someone run alongside him to learn, watch, and grow. He wrote to the Corinthians, "I am sending to you Timothy, my son whom I love, who is faithful in the Lord. He will remind you of my way of life in Christ Jesus, which agrees with what I teach everywhere in every church" (1 Corinthians 4:17). The portion of this verse that always strikes me is the middle part: "he will remind you of my way of life in Christ Jesus." The desire of a mentor is not to produce a mini-clone but rather to endorse an individual, as the Flows did for me.

Why do you think colleges desire to hire assistant coaches who serve under great head coaches? Those assistants learned from the best. A great head coach will know his staff well enough to know how he can help each one of his staff attain his goals. I am still reveling in the fact that Wake Forest made it to the Orange Bowl in 2007. Even though our head coach, Jim Grobe, unequivocally stated that he desired to stay put, he continually stated that other schools would be crazy not to look at his assistants to serve as head coaches. Soon thereafter some of his assistant coaches were offered wonderful coaching opportunities. Mentors see what others might not see and do their best to harvest the gold within.

SEASONED ADVICE

Walter C. Wright Jr., sixty-three; executive director of the DePree Leadership Center, Pasadena, CA:

When I look back to the first third of my life from the perspective now of the third third, I am not sure I would do it very differently. I might make better choices given what I now know, but my basic philosophy of life has not changed. Early on I learned five important truths. First I learned the value of seeking out mentors—wise men and women who will ask you the questions that keep you focused on who you intend to be. My early mentors walked into my life unannounced, and they taught me how important the mentoring relationship is, and I was not far into my first third before I started seeking out mentors. Second, I discovered early that the trail is more important than the summits. Because I had sons while still in my twenties, I learned to relax about getting places and to enjoy the day at hand. It took me a bit longer than my peers to finish each stage of my schooling, but along the way I had marvelous opportunities to practice much of what I was studying, to enjoy my family, and to climb mountains with friends.

The most important advice I would give any person early in the journey is to avoid rushing! Tomorrow will still be there. Live today; enjoy the people whom God sends across your path today; learn from them; care for them. The journey of life happens each day, and life is measured by the journey we walk, not how high or how far we can go. The next three truths formed the core of a simple philosophy that has guided my life as long as I can remember. I want to be able to answer the following three questions in the affirmative every day: Am I making a contribution? Am I learning something? Am I having fun? With those five truths I continue to enjoy life, think about what I want to learn next, and wait to see what God will send across my trail.

SEASONED ADVICE

Thelma Wells, sixty-five; president of Women of God Ministries; founder of Daughters of Zion Leadership Mentoring Program; author and speaker at Women of Faith Conferences; Dallas:

I entered the banking profession in 1972 and began teaching banking in 1978. Little did I know that this was a stepping-stone to what I would eventually do and what I was called to do: speaking for a living. While teaching, I noticed that too many people in my classes had such low self-esteem. I prayed and asked God to give me something that I could say to motivate, inspire, influence, and empower them for the rest of their lives, even if they forgot my name and my face. As I walked into my church one afternoon, a friend noticed a little bumblebee I was wearing on my shoulder. "Thelma Wells, that sure is a pretty bee, and every time you wear that bee, remember, you can bee the best of what you want to be." After studying the plight of the bumblebee, I realized that it defies the laws of aeronautical science by flying in spite of its limitations. Similarly, people determine how high they fly by overcoming obstacles and limitations on their way to success.

POINTS TO PONDER

1. Take a minute to write down the names of those individuals in your life who have mentored you.
2. Next to their names, write down one or two things you learned from each person.
3. If you have not done so recently, write a short note thanking one of your mentors for the impact he or she has had on your life.

NOTES

1. Walter C. Wright, *Mentoring: The Promise of Relational Leadership* (Carlisle, UK: Paternoster Press, 2004), p. 16.

19

THE IMPORTANCE OF DISCIPLINE

Dallas Willard defines "a discipline for the spiritual life [as], when the dust of history is blown away, nothing but an activity undertaken to bring us into more effective cooperation with Christ and his Kingdom."[1] Discipline is not a skill set that comes easy to most of us, and yet there is an innate freedom found within a disciplined life. Familiarity with a routine offers profound freedom. Similar to spiritual disciplines, a handful of practical disciplines in the workplace has served me well through the years.

DISCIPLINE OF DILIGENCE

The advent of the Internet, coupled with the old standard, television, has made wasting time an art form. J. Oswald Sanders asserts, "Leaders will work while others waste time, study while others snooze, pray while others daydream. Slothful habits are overcome, whether in thought, deed or dress."[2] When I was younger, if I was too lazy to mow the grass or fix the back door, my dad would inevitably get around to it. Now that I am an adult, the rafters sag and the house leaks when I'm lazy (see Ecclesiastes 10:18). Procrastination is my enemy. I do my best to touch papers once, return communications in a timely fashion, and stick to the task in front of me. The author of Ecclesiastes challenges you to "sow your seed in the morning, and at evening let not your hands be idle, for you do not know which will succeed, whether this or that, or whether both will do equally well" (11:6).

DISCIPLINE TO HOLD YOUR TONGUE

"The words of a gossip are like choice morsels; they go down to a man's inmost parts" (Proverbs 18:8). Holding my tongue is a discipline in progress. Why is it that knowing all the details of a juicy situation is so tempting? At times I may veil the pursuit of gossip under the umbrella of "I'm just trying to help," but in truth I just desire to know. We encounter people every day whom we know we can trust with information and those whom we know we cannot trust. Hopefully we can be trusted. In every working environment it is critical to surmise the situation and to avoid those who talk too much because inevitably those individuals will betray you (Proverbs 20:19). If a person shares information about someone who is not present, why wouldn't that same person betray you when you are not around?

DISCIPLINE OF HANDWRITING NOTES

My mother has always modeled the importance of appreciating people with the written word. During my first year in college, I received handwritten notes from my mother three to four times a week. Handwritten notes show people you care enough to write your thoughts on paper, address an envelope, put a stamp on it, and drop it in the mail. In short, you honor people with your time and affirmation. When I was soliciting contributions for seasoned advice for my earlier book, *Perspectives*, I was very impressed with Steve Reinemund, the former CEO of Pepsico. Even though he was unable to contribute, he cared enough to handwrite me a short note offering his best thoughts. It was only a line or two, but he clearly demonstrated by his actions that he valued me. E-mails are wonderful, but there's still something special about receiving a piece of mail with your name on it.

DISCIPLINE OF NOTE-TAKING

The older I get, the more I realize the importance of writing things down. Sometimes I even write down where I write things down. The story goes that one of Albert Einstein's colleagues asked for his phone number, and Einstein reached for a telephone directory. It's been said that he never memorized anything that it could take him less than two minutes to look up.[3] Most leaders I know have a catch-all book—a notebook in which to write down thoughts, directives, insights, or reminders. I have one notebook for work and one notebook for home (www.levenger.com has high-quality notebooks). My work notebook contains a compilation of checklists, important phone numbers, cryptic notes of phone conversations, ideas, and quick reminders separated by horizontal slashes. For the checklists, I use a red pen to mark off completed items. In contrast, my home notebook is used primarily for journaling, note-taking at church or elsewhere, and any other creative thoughts, stories, or memories I desire to record.

DISCIPLINE OF EXPANDING YOUR VOCABULARY

Make it a practice to stop and look up any word the meaning of which is unclear. Expanding your vocabulary continually sharpens your mind. If you do not own a dictionary, spend a few dollars and purchase one.

DISCIPLINE OF PUNCTUALITY

A few years ago the former assistant press secretary to President George W. Bush, Reid Dickens, told our students a story highlighting the importance of punctuality. Dickens was told that a flight would depart at a specified time. When he arrived one minute late, the flight had left. Be on time for appointments, conference calls, your daughter's recital, *everything*. Punctuality honors others. Tardiness indirectly says, "My time is more valuable than your time."

DISCIPLINE OF READING

As the son of a lifelong reading specialist, I have always had a book at my fingertips. If you are not reading consistently, more than likely you are not growing. Reading engages your mind on a different level than any other medium. For many years now I have voraciously consumed handfuls of Christian nonfiction books, but I have been convicted to expand my reading spectrum and read all types of books. Reading only one genre of book pigeonholes your thinking. Ignite your mind by dipping into the classics or reading your favorite poet. While reading, implement a system to easily reference particularly poignant passages. I make small vertical hash marks next to passages, flip to the back of the book, and write the page number as well as a word or two to easily reference the passage.

DISCIPLINE OF SLEEP

"How long will you lie there, you sluggard? When will you get up from your sleep? A little sleep, a little slumber, a little folding of the hands to rest—and poverty will come on you like a bandit and scarcity like an armed man" (Proverbs 6:9-11). Sleep is important. Most of us do not get enough sleep, though some of us get way too much. Honor your employer by arriving to work well-rested. Lack of sleep greatly contributes to ineffectiveness.

DISCIPLINE OF DRESSING APPROPRIATELY

In order to be treated as a professional, you must dress as a professional. Most working environments include a dress code. Abide by it! Do not revert back to your adolescence, trying to see how far you can push the imaginary line. Your colleagues will secretly resent you, and your superiors will label you as a usurper of authority.

DISCIPLINE OF REMEMBERING NAMES

The sweetest sound to almost everyone is the sound of his or her own name. A few years ago a man would introduce himself to me and ask my name every time I saw him. Each time my bruised ego would remember the previous times we had met. To my friends, it became a recurring joke because to this man I was deemed unworthy of remembering. In contrast, my headmaster successfully sets out to know every single person's name in our entire K–12 school. He knows the value of honoring someone by simply remembering his or her name. Here's a helpful hint for those challenged in this area: if you do not know a person's name, simply ask someone who does before you approach that person and reinforce the name in your memory by referring to the person by name often when conversing with him or her.

SEASONED ADVICE

Marc Khedouri, forty-three; dean of students at Wesleyan School, Norcross, GA:

As the dean of students, I am the focal point of our discipline system, but it is a shared responsibility with the faculty. When I describe my responsibilities to people, I usually get an odd look, and many comment something along the lines of "Well, someone has to do that, and better you than me." I admit that administering discipline is a peculiar calling; essentially, though, I see my role as the person most responsible for bringing out the best in each and every student. Rules and boundaries help cultivate self-discipline, which is the intended goal of our discipline system. Roy Baumeister, a psychologist at Case Western University, has found that "self-control is a better predictor of 'life outcomes,' career success, well-being than is IQ." Think about that for a second: self-discipline is more essential to achieving one's goals than intelligence, a statement both revolutionary and true. The very best I can do for young people is to hold them accountable, lovingly but firmly.

From my perspective, discipline is not what you do *to* someone but rather what you do *for* someone. It may well be the highest form of love, for it says in effect, "I care about you enough to only accept your best, and this is not it." I often remind students that the purpose of our rules is to cultivate self-discipline, apart from which they are unlikely to become successful. In our culture, discipline often has negative connotations, but I believe it is the vehicle through which we teach young people lessons that cannot be learned any other way. I think about all these things every day as I fulfill my responsibilities here at school. I know most people may not have an approach as thoughtful, but our work here is important. I never want to give up on a child, and I know the lessons we are seeking to impart will make our students more pleasing in God's sight and more productive people. In Proverbs we are told, "train a child in the way he should go, and when he is old he will not turn from it." There is no greater gift we can give others than the ability to control themselves and to do that which is pleasing in God's sight.

POINTS TO PONDER

1. Who is the most disciplined person you know? What do you admire about this person?
2. Read 1 Corinthians 9:24–27.
3. How did Paul approach discipline?
4. In what areas in your own life do you desire more discipline?

NOTES

1. Dallas Willard, *The Spirit of the Disciplines* (New York: Harper San Francisco, 1991), p. 156.
2. J. Oswald Sanders, *Spiritual Leadership* (Chicago: Moody Press, 1994), p. 53.
3. See http://oaks.nvg.org/sa5ra17.html; accessed June 27, 2006.

20

THE IMPORTANCE OF
SKILL

In the little town of Lumberjack, Michigan, a small lumber business owner decided to orchestrate a contest among his employees in order to motivate them. Even though most of his business was mechanized, he thought everyone would enjoy a day of reverting back to the days of his grandfather when chain saws were nonexistent. The ground rules were simple: the winner would be whoever chopped down the most trees between 9 A.M. and 3 P.M. Everyone reveled in the opportunity to set aside their monotonous tasks for a chance to win the Remington Chain Saw 5000—a beautiful piece of handiwork not sold in stores. Needless to say, the men puffed up their chests, all the while barking out their intended tree totals. Most people had their money on Jumbo Joe—a rather large man with a barrel chest and biceps the size of most men's thighs. Jumbo Joe reeked of confidence and raw power; as a result, most assumed they were competing for second place.

On the morning of the contest, a number of competitors had dropped out, and one woman had been added to the list. Maddie was a tough cookie. She rowed for Princeton and was home for the summer in order to make some additional money. Everyone praised Maddie for entering the contest, but under their breath they believed she had no chance of winning. Honestly, how could a woman compete with Jumbo Joe? Around 8:45 the owner set out the axes and explained the rules once again to the contestants. At 9 o'clock the contestants scattered to their assigned areas. After the first hour, the owner drove around to check in on his employees. Most of the employees were making good progress, but Jumbo Joe and Maddie stood out from the rest. Jumbo Joe had chopped down nearly twice as many trees as his competitors, and the owner found Maddie sitting on a log sharpening her axe.

Another few hours passed, and the owner went out once again to check on their progress. By midday Maddie had caught up to Jumbo Joe, and lactic acid was beginning to seize Jumbo Joe's massive biceps. Even though he towered over Maddie, she took half as many swings in order to bring down a tree. By the end of the day, Maddie easily took home the Remington Chain Saw 5000. Amazed by her victory, the local papers interviewed her to ask her how she did it. Maddie simply quoted Ecclesiastes 10:10: "If the ax is dull and its edge unsharpened, more strength is needed but skill will bring success." An abundance of skill does not guarantee success, but it certainly increases your chances.

A few years ago I traveled to Tegucigalpa, Honduras to visit some friends at the Micah House—a ministry that supports, trains, and develops street kids to adulthood. As the pilot began his descent toward the airport, I could tell many of the passengers were becoming somewhat restless. This was my first visit to Honduras, so I attributed their restlessness to first-time flying jitters. Shortly afterward, the pilot barely avoided some mountains, plummeted to the runway, slammed on the brakes, and turned the plane sharply upon landing. All around me people were cheering, and numerous people were crossing themselves in thanksgiving for a successful landing. Little did I know that this airport stands on a plateau in the basin of several mountains, has one of the shortest international runways in the world, and contains a slight slope that makes braking difficult and comes to an end on a cliff that forces the pilots to simultaneously land and slow down skillfully enough to turn the corner without flipping the plane.

Needless to say, I was not surprised when I learned that only a handful of pilots in the world can land at this airport. Only a few pilots are skillful enough to know these surroundings, know their instruments, and have the confidence to take on this daunting challenge. Drs. Thomas Addington and Stephen Graves define skill as "understanding something completely and transforming that knowledge into creations of wonder and excellence."[1] Skill does not guarantee success, but I was certainly glad my pilot was skillful in his vocation.

As Christians, we are continually called to perfect the gifts God has given us. A familiar parable in Scripture, the parable of the talents, illustrates this point quite well. In the parable, before the master left on a journey he gave his servants talents (money) to use for his good: "To one he gave five talents of money, to another two talents, and to another one talent, *each according to his ability*" (Matthew 25:15, emphasis added). In the same way, each of us is gifted in an area or two, and some people, by God's grace, are gifted in multiple areas. These servants handled their entrusted gifts in different ways. The servant with five talents doubled his net worth, as did the servant with two talents, but the servant with one talent "dug a hole in the ground and hid his master's money" (Matthew 25:18).

Eventually the master came back to settle his accounts. To the first two servants he replied, "Well done, good and faithful servant! You have been faithful with a few things; I will put you in charge of many things. Come and share your master's happiness!" (Matthew 25:21, 23). Unfortunately for the last servant, his master did not agree with his plan, calling him a "wicked, lazy servant" (Matthew 25:26). As a result, his master took his talent from him and gave it to the one with ten talents. What can we learn from this parable about skill?

First, *God expects us to enhance our skill set.* In the parable the two servants who worked to increase their talents were praised for their efforts. At the end of the parable Matthew offers, "For everyone who has will be given more" (25:29). Much like our definition of skill, God understands the importance of understanding something completely. Each person's vocation will differ on how to do this. In most fields, there are minimum requirements in order to keep one's certification, but God desires more. If God calls you to a certain arena, He desires your continual growth. Stretch yourself. Look for growth opportunities. Professional development should rank high on your list of priorities. In our credential-laden society, you may often need to work backwards. What is your ultimate goal? Where do you feel God is leading you? What criteria do you need in order to fill that role? Do your homework. If you know you'll need an advanced degree, don't drag your feet; go get it. Do not continually hit your head on the proverbial glass ceiling because you were lazy in your youth.

Second, *God understands our limits.* In looking at this parable again, I was struck by the master's decision to use the exact same wording in verses 21 and 23. Both servants started with a different amount of talents, both doubled their talents, and yet the master experienced the same joy with their result. God desires for us to do the best with what we've been given. The older I get, the more fully I comprehend that God designed each person with a purpose. Through human lenses, it might not seem fair that God gave a particular person so many gifts, but the expectations for all of us are the same regardless of how many gifts the Lord has given us. He desires for us to transform our knowledge into creations of wonder and excellence. What does your product look like? Are you proud of your creation?

Finally, *God desires to reward us with more kingdom responsibility*. Skill does not guarantee success, but if you continually enhance the gifts the Lord has given you, God will provide you with more opportunities to serve Him. Be faithful in the small things so God can trust you with big things. "Do you see a man skilled in his work? He will serve before kings; he will not serve before obscure men" (Proverbs 22:29).

Until recent centuries most young people lacked options for their career paths. Jesus apprenticed as a carpenter because His earthly father was a carpenter. If your dad was a farmer, you were a farmer. If your dad was a fisherman, you were a fisherman. Gary Badcock suggests, "The New Testament, for example, not only does not consider the question of vocation in terms of 'career choice,' but it could not have done so, for such a question would have been virtually unintelligible to its original audience."[2] Thankfully, we have more options today. In this volatile job market, a way to differentiate yourself from others is to continually enhance your skill set. Be the best in the arena to which the Lord has called you. Do not rest on your laurels.

SEASONED ADVICE

Shaunti Feldhahn, thirty-nine; best-selling author (www.shaunti. com), public speaker, and nationally syndicated newspaper columnist; Atlanta:

One of the most underrated skills in the market at large is writing, regardless of your field. People find themselves in great demand when they can take a thought or a complex bit of information and cull it down to its very essence in order to communicate a simple truth clearly. And that process also, frankly, hones your analytical skills. As one of my graduate school professors once put it, "You don't truly understand something until you can write it down."

It's interesting that although I've built up a skill in writing now, I was never a particularly good writer in previous years. In fact, at nearly every stage of my career before this one—on Wall Street, on Capitol Hill, and at graduate school—nearly every evaluation highlighted my need to improve my writing abilities! I actually learned how to write well while at the Kennedy School at Harvard—they focused on that *a lot* because they knew that by teaching someone to write well, they also were teaching that person how to think.

As a newspaper columnist, I am charged with the daunting task of whittling down an immense amount of information into a few paragraphs. I continually force myself to ask the hard question, what is the core issue? This sounds like a cliché, but it's very true: this takes lots of practice, over and over and over. Some of my models for good writers are senior assistants to government officials. These men and women must deal with complex issues from every possible angle and then offer their concise recommendations. They have to take five hundred pages worth of important information and present the policymaker with the five most important bullet points that they need to make a decision. There is no room for extraneous information. I actually believe the lack of extraneous information in my books has been the tipping point. I've done my best to remove all the information that readers have already heard and only offer them new information, the surprises they didn't already know.

With the success of my books, and getting so incredibly busy, I have had to focus my life even more. I heeded the advice of a friend who told me, "Focus on the items only you can do; pass off everything else to others." This advice has freed me up to focus on the big items in my life: only I can write and speak with my specific message, and only I can be a mom to my kids. Even though I travel quite a bit, my family comes first. For example, I make it a point to mark my calendar very early so I can attend my daughter's field trips. Maintaining healthy boundaries is always challenging, but I feel like I am doing what I was built to do.

Scripture often tells us that crowds were amazed at the "authority" of the teachings of people like Paul, Peter, and, of course, Jesus. I never fully understood what that meant until I started speaking myself. It's like God does something supernatural through me, and people who hear it find themselves thinking, *That's exactly right.* When I am speaking in front of hundreds or thousands of women, I can actually *watch* and see their eyes being opened to what God wants them to know. The most common comment I hear is something like, "My husband has been trying to tell me that for years, and I never believed him, but now I do."

I am so, so humbled to watch how the Lord is using me in spite of my weaknesses and insecurities. It is a powerful feeling to feel like I'm almost watching from the sidelines like everyone else as God moves.

POINTS TO PONDER

1. Where do you feel God has gifted you the most?
2. In what tangible ways are you improving your skill set?
3. How have you seen God bless your efforts?

NOTES

1. Thomas Addington and Stephen Graves, *A Case for Skill* (Fayetteville, AR: Cornerstone Alliance, 1997), p. xv.
2. Gary D. Badcock, *The Way of Life* (Grand Rapids, MI: Eerdmans, 1998), pp. 41–42.

21

THE IMPORTANCE OF HUMILITY

As I was flying back from St. Louis a few years ago, two teens (a brother and sister traveling alone) sat across the aisle from me. The flight was delayed, and the siblings became restless. This restlessness manifested itself in various forms, such as hitting, smacking, and blowing on one another. At first most passengers found their playfulness endearing, but after thirty minutes of excessive adolescent behavior, a man sitting directly in front of them turned around and reprimanded them. Evidently his words rang hollow because he had to call in reinforcements—the flight attendant. He succinctly explained the situation, and her maternal instincts emerged as she addressed the children. "Do you have your papers for traveling?" asked the flight attendant in a sweet voice. "The lady said we didn't need them . . ." Interrupting, the flight attendant replied, "Because you are over twelve, correct? And as a result you are considered adults. So act like adults."

Although her words were harsh, the message echoed in my ears. How is our behavior any different during this time when we're not yet home with our Father? Communion with

165

our Father serves as the essential tool in guiding, directing, and shaping our feet of clay. Pride is a critical roadblock in thinking anything to the contrary. Ralph Waldo Emerson once said, "A great man is always willing to be little."[1]

Unfortunately, in the working world "willing to be little" is not always a praised character trait. How else will others know how wonderful we are if we do not share our wonderful accomplishments? The challenge of remaining humble dates back to the early days of the Bible. In the book of Esther, Haman was elevated by King Xerxes to a "seat of honor higher than that of all the other nobles. All the royal officials at the king's gate knelt down and paid honor to Haman. . . . But Mordecai would not kneel down or pay him honor" (Esther 3:1–2). As a result, Haman loathed Mordecai, a Jew, and pledged not only to kill Mordecai but all of his people as well. Fearing for his life and those of the Jews, Mordecai solicited help from Queen Esther, also a Jew, who approached Xerxes and "touched the tip of the scepter" (Esther 5:2). This prompted Xerxes to ask Esther, "What is your request? Even up to half the kingdom, it will be given you" (Esther 5:3).

Cleverly, Esther held her cards close to her vest and requested a banquet with Xerxes and Haman at which she would fully answer the king's question. Not surprisingly, Haman puffed up his chest and boasted to friends and family that he was "the only person Queen Esther invited to accompany the king to the banquet" (Esther 5:12). For some reason, the night before the banquet Xerxes was restless and could not sleep; so he asked a servant to read to him from the official records. He thus learned that Mordecai had exposed two conspirators earlier who wanted to kill the king, but Mordecai had received no honor for this feat. Xerxes solicited advice from Haman asking, "What should be done for the man the king delights to honor?" (Esther 6:6). Haman, full of his own self-worth, assumed the king was speaking about him; so he described a lavish display. After Haman's enthusiastic response, the king commanded Haman to "get the robe and the horse and do just as you have suggested for Mordecai the Jew, who sits at the king's gate. Do not neglect anything you have recommended" (Esther 6:10). Crushed, Haman's downfall continued as Esther declared Haman the enemy of her people and Xerxes chose to hang Haman on the same gallows Haman had prepared for Mordecai.

A friend of mine once said, "You're never as good as people say you are, and you're never as bad either." Unfortunately, the first part of that statement proves to be the hang-up for most of us. It's hard not to believe others' praises. Haman's pride led to his downfall. Living counterculturally in today's world is never easy, but every so often the world provides us with some tangible examples. In 1994 the now Hall of Famer Ryne Sandberg felt as though he was not living up to his huge contract. He explains, "I'm not the type of person who can leave my game at the ballpark feeling comfortable my future is set regardless of my performance. I'm certainly not the type of person who can ask the Cubs and Cubs fans to pay my salary when I'm not happy with my mental approach and performance."[2] As a result, Sandberg walked away from over ten million dollars and retired early. He eventually came back to finish out his career, but the point is not lost on me.

Even though I'm a lifelong St. Louis Cardinals fan, I admire Sandberg's ability to humble himself enough to recognize it wasn't just about him. He had a responsibility to his fans as well as to the ownership of the team. I do not know Sandberg's religious beliefs, but he clearly modeled the charge that "whoever wants to become great among you must be your servant" (Matthew 20:26). The following techniques help me continually remind myself to strive for a spirit of humility.

Wear a non-defensive spirit. By nature I am a very prideful person, and when confronted, I find it difficult to adorn a non-defensive spirit. Casting aside a spirit of defensiveness, however, Chuck Swindoll tells us, "reveals a willingness to be accountable. Genuine humility operates on a rather simple philosophy: Nothing to prove, Nothing to lose."[3]

Serve others. Every year my school gives an award for a faculty member who willingly and selflessly serves others. I should never ever get this award. I am extremely selfish with my time, and whether spoken or implied, I always think to myself, *What's in it for me?* Thus I face a continual internal struggle to acknowledge others' needs and to actively decide to meet their needs. Serving others requires personal sacrifice as well as the humility to consider others more important than yourself (Philippians 2:3).

Maintain a healthy view of your limits. None of us is irreplaceable. I know I would like to think that if I left my job, the wheels would fall off and everyone would smear ashes on their faces and run around in burlap bags, but God raises up people for a time and then calls them elsewhere. "Niebuhr beckons us to accept what we cannot change, to take on with excellence what we can change and to recognize the difference between the two. This is not fatalism; it is humility."[4]

SEASONED ADVICE

Rome Hartman, fifty; former executive producer for CBS Evening News, *New York City:*

I often quote Ephesians 6:7, which tells us to "Serve wholeheartedly, as if you were serving the Lord, not men." My wife Amy sometimes says I use this as an excuse to be a workaholic, and she's probably right. But I've always taken it as a charge to work as hard and as well as possible, as an indication that such effort and excellence can be pleasing to God. Not that I remotely think God spends much time worrying about what goes on the *Evening News* each night; it's more about not squandering the gifts He has given me and not wasting my calling. Think about the incredibly intricate and powerful brains God went to the trouble to give each of us. He didn't have to do it. He must have wanted us to at least try to use as much of that brainpower as possible. To let such a gift go to waste seems an insult. Similarly, those folks whose work involves physical labor are putting to use the incredible machine that is the human body taking direction from the brain, another gift from God.

Of course, it's not enough to work hard and seek excellence. We also have to figure out how to always hold onto humility in the process, to understand that if we're doing well, making good decisions, winning the race, it's not about us. Just once, when something turns out really well at work, try this out: give credit to the people on your team, particularly the junior people, who've been working hard to make *you* look good. Do it publicly, in a staff meeting, or do it privately, with e-mails or brief handwritten notes to those folks. Tell them that you understand how important they are to making the whole place run right; tell them that you're grateful. Grace just isn't expected in the workplace sometimes; it surprises people. In a staff meeting a couple of months ago, when we had a reason to celebrate, I took just a minute to note the hard work of my predecessor, who'd left the job under difficult circumstances. That wasn't for show; it was sincere. Even if he hadn't been ultimately successful, he'd had a hand in beginning the thing we were celebrating that day. I had no idea that would get much of a reaction; it just seemed like the right thing to say. But several people came up to me afterward to say they'd been *floored* when I said it; they just weren't accustomed to such generosity and humility, they said. Small things can be big. Hard work is bigger.

POINTS TO PONDER

1. Look up the following verses: John 3:30; 1 Corinthians 15:9; Ephesians 3:8; 1 Timothy 1:15.

CAREER

2. In what areas in your life do you struggle with humility?

3. "A leader's humility should grow with the passing of years, like other attitudes and qualities."[5] Would others say your humility has increased or decreased with the passing years?

NOTES

1. This quotation can be found at http://www.brainyquote.com/quotes/quotes/r/ralphwaldo130654.html.

2. Steve Marantz, "Light Footprints in the Sand—Ryne Sandberg's Retirement," *The Sporting News*, June 27, 1994, p. 3; http://www.findarticles.com/p/articles/mi_m1208/is_n26_v217/ai_15510194.

3. Chuck Swindoll, *Improving Your Serve* (Nashville: W Publishing Group, 1981), p. 25

4. Gordon T. Smith, *Courage and Calling* (Downers Grove, IL: InterVarsity Press, 1999), p. 174.

5. J. Oswald Sanders, *Spiritual Leadership* (Chicago: Moody Press, 1994), p. 61.

22

THE IMPORTANCE OF WEIGHING YOUR WORDS

Years ago children would write their deepest, darkest secrets in their diary and safeguard their thoughts with a lock and key. My sister would hide her diary somewhere in her room, hoping I wouldn't find the mystery to her soul—as if a ten-year-old girl has any mystery to her soul. Today some individuals choose to post their thoughts on the Internet for all to see even though, amazingly enough, most people do not recognize that their posts, blogs, or web sites may cause them to be expelled from college, lose a job opportunity, or even be thrown in jail. Googling someone is commonplace and oftentimes is the first stop for commandeering endless amounts of information. *Business Week* suggests that "googling people is also becoming a way for bosses and headhunters to do continuous and stealthy background checks on employees, no disclosure required. Google is an end run around discrimination laws, inasmuch as employers can find out all manner of information . . . that is legally off limits in interviews."[1] Be careful what you put in print.

For most of us though, the most common way of printed

communication is e-mail. At one time or another each of us has said something we regretted, but in the electronic world our words are not so easily erased. You never know where that e-mail will end up once you send it. Unfortunately, I have had to learn my lessons the hard way. There's the colleague who chooses to forward your e-mail to countless others when you only intended it for his or her eyes. There's the time you forget to erase the bottom of an e-mail where one colleague berates the colleague to whom you are forwarding the e-mail. Do not kid yourself—everyone always scrolls all the way down. In the ideal world all of us would have enough willpower to only read the portion that is sent to us, but inevitably curiosity gets the best of us, and we justify our actions under the umbrella of "there could be pertinent information below that will help clarify the situation." In some cases, it is true, but inevitably we are just nosy. "All man's efforts are for his mouth, yet his appetite is never satisfied" (Ecclesiastes 6:7). This is not only true of our physical appetite. E-mail is a wonderful mode of communication, but in order to navigate the land mines surrounding e-mails, the following suggestions may prove helpful:

Professional/private accounts. Do your best to keep your private e-mails and professional e-mails completely separate. I have two primary accounts, and over the years the distinction has grown a little more blurry, but it still remains very helpful.

Allow a cooling-off period. Oftentimes we react to a situation or an e-mail before collecting our thoughts or potentially gathering all of the necessary facts. Assuming you have already written the e-mail, wait. Take time to think of the consequences of your e-mail. Potentially shelf the e-mail overnight or have someone you trust review the e-mail and gauge his or her reaction. "When words are many, sin is not absent, but he who holds his tongue is wise" (Proverbs 10:19).

Is e-mail the best option? Face-to-face interaction proves more effective to resolve conflict and diffuse situations.

Weigh your words. If you must use mail, remember that "a gentle answer turns away wrath, but a harsh word stirs up anger" (Proverbs 15:1). Keep in mind that there are consequences to your actions. Are you ready to accept the consequences for what you put in print?

Paper trail. E-mail is a wonderful vehicle to track information. BCC (Blind Carbon Copy) yourself on all pertinent e-mails, and file them away in a safe location or simply move the sent e-mail to a file folder. On numerous occasions I have referenced old e-mails in order to solidify my case.

Remember e-mail etiquette.

- *Tone.* The biggest downfall of e-mail is the inability of the reader to assess tone. For instance, I had to instruct my mother on the proper use of exclamation points. She started e-mailing later in life and loved using forty to fifty exclamation points in e-mails to show her excitement. Unfortunately, she did not realize that at times exclamation points and/or all caps typically convey shouting as well. Our headmaster always encourages us to speak with a parent in person or, if not possible, on the phone to share tough information. Sympathy is much easier to read in a person's facial expressions than in the written word.

- *Length.* Be careful how much you write, for "as a dream comes when there are many cares, so the speech of a fool when there are many words" (Ecclesiastes 5:3). For many years I felt the necessity to respond with a similar length as the sender. Obviously you do not want to offend the sender with a short, curt response, but oftentimes a loquacious e-mail does not require a response of equal length. In professional e-mails, address the appropriate need in as few words as possible.

- *Grammar.* The written word is a reflection of what you value. Be sure to proofread all e-mails. When I worked in college admissions, e-mails from prospective students would amaze me. Individuals with 700+ verbal scores would write e-mails with sloppy grammar.

In admissions, every contact is evaluated. As stated above, unfortunately you never know where the e-mail may end up, and it is important to always use tact, grace, and care in all written correspondences.

• *Response.* Respond in an appropriate length of time. Assuming the request is not time-sensitive, the next day is normally appropriate, although, if possible, same-day responses are highly appreciated. If you know it will take a day or so to gather the necessary information, pass that along to the inquirer.

Over my lifetime my words have landed me in numerous precarious situations. If you know, like me, that you are predisposed to making errors in judgment in the electronic world, take time to think through each correspondence and the words you will use. "A man of knowledge uses words with restraint, and a man of understanding is even-tempered" (Proverbs 17:27).

SEASONED ADVICE

Paul M. Barclay Sr., fifty-two; commercial real estate and development, mentor; Winston-Salem, NC:

As a person who has studied and practiced many of the martial arts for a long time, I have come to discover one of the most powerful weapons in the world. This weapon is not held, sold, thrown, or shot, nor is it something only Jack Bauer possesses. The weapon is words. When you think of great communicators, they all seem to call us to believe in ourselves or our cause. Each of these folks use words to call us to action, never to passivity. Some combat is open and easy to identify; other combat is covert and hidden from view. Both types are equally as damaging and can provide the same results. Combat is merely conflict raised up a notch. Combat is not only violent action; it can be a war of words.

My friends know I have to quote or reference movies in about anything I do. Movies often illustrate what I cannot. In a recent football movie, *Invincible*, the audience enters into the real-life story of Vince Papale. Vince is a married, middle-aged schoolteacher and part-time bartender. He is a lifetime Philadelphia Eagles football fan and season ticket holder for a historically losing team. In a brief snapshot of his life, we see him lose his teaching job and his wife. She not only leaves him and takes everything with her but also leaves a powerful note (more on that later). Given the closely knit area in which they live, everyone in the neighborhood knows what has happened.

Vince's childhood buddy, Johnny, is afraid of nearly everything, especially anyone succeeding at anything and leaving the neighborhood, and he condemns anyone who thinks differently than he does or tries to leave. He attempts to convince Vince of his twisted notions. As the movie moves along, the Philadelphia Eagles decide to have a tryout open to the public. It would seem that every oddball, football wannabe heads to the stadium. It is a riot. Vince is the star of his backyard league; so his pals encourage him to try out. To everyone's surprise, he survives the tryout and is asked to work out with the team at training camp. He is way out of his league but fights to do his best. He frequently reads the note his wife left him, now placed at the top of his locker. That note read: "Vince . . . You'll never go anywhere . . . You'll never make any money . . . and you'll never make a name for yourself." This note seemed to drive him harder and further than the other players.

In my experience, words are capable of only two results: (1) They can drive and encourage us to action. Or (2) they can wound and paralyze us. How many of us still believe a demeaning nickname or story about us from our childhood? I believe words are never neutral or inert. I see us as people called to yield the golden sword of words for good and not for evil. We are charged to encourage folks to freedom, forgiveness, hope, courage, love, to use words that "spur one another on toward love

175

and good deeds" (Hebrews 10:24), to bless and not condemn. How do your words affect others? Imagine what you would attempt to do if you knew you couldn't fail. Would your life and actions look different?

POINTS TO PONDER

1. What e-mail lesson have you had to learn the hard way?
2. What is your e-mail pet peeve?
3. What measures do you have in place to weigh your words?

RESOURCES

1. For a quick reference guide to help you with e-mail etiquette, see www.emailreplies.com.
2. One of countless free e-mail systems to help you differentiate your personal e-mails from your professional e-mails is www.mail.yahoo.com.

NOTES

1. Michelle Conlin, "You Are What You Post: Bosses Are Using Google to Peer into Places Job Interviews Can't Take Them," *Business Week*, March 27, 2006, p. 52.

23

THE IMPORTANCE OF FAMILY

I recently returned from my grandmother's funeral. She was eighty-seven and had been in failing health for the last few years. Her husband of sixty-four years bathed her, cooked for her, and managed every other aspect of the household until her needs became too much. Last week she passed on with her husband and three sons by her bedside to say good-bye. Grandma Creel was my first familial loss. Prior to the funeral, we sat around in their living room with their retired pastor, Reverend Lehman. The spry eighty-year-old man with a resonating voice talked about my grandma and asked what she had meant to all of us. Needless to say, many tears were shed and tissues were dispensed, but what struck me the most was the importance of family. How blessed my grandparents were to have three sons who were devoted to them.

As a child, we would always go to Grandma's house for Christmas—always. Everyone was expected to reconvene each year or else. I imagine that expectation was hard on my mother, but for me it was wonderful. I loved the tradition of driving up to Chicago after school, stopping at McDonald's, and keeping my eyes peeled for the first signs of snow or, even better, Santa Claus. Their house was on a few acres of land on the outskirts of town. My heart would palpitate more quickly as soon as I saw the white fence around the perimeter of their home. Their dog, an American Eskimo named Vodka, would lovingly meet us at the door. Their house was decorated from floor to ceiling with crazy Christmas creations. Christmas was Grandma's favorite holiday. She loved us so much that she would even drape herself in a Santa Claus outfit. As the evening grew long, our parents would warn us that Santa Claus would not visit our house unless we were in bed. Minutes later we would watch Santa Claus with parcels in tow race past our house in the backyard. Watching Santa Claus pass your house on Christmas always seemed to motivate us little ones to scurry off to bed.

The resonating theme after she passed was her desire to always place family first. When my dad, as a young man, had an internship in downtown Chicago, she would always wake up at 4:30 A.M. to ensure he had a large breakfast before his day. Another theme that emerged was her iron will. She always, sometimes to a fault, protected her three sons whether or not they were right. Her sons always desired to honor her in everything they did, but like most young men, each had his shortfalls. In his youth, my dad was known to smoke a little bit, but he respected my grandmother too much to ever smoke in front of her. One time while he was mowing the neighbors' yard across town, he decided to light up a cigarette; to his surprise, she popped by to say hello. My grandmother swore he swallowed the cigarette because it miraculously disappeared when he saw her. They never talked about the incident. My mom shared that Grandma's iron will came in handy when she had a task at hand; nothing could dissuade her. For instance, at one of my sister's first dance recitals, my grandmother wanted to give my sister flowers after the performance. For a variety of reasons, this appeared to be impossible, but my grandmother made it happen; she put family first.

As the matriarch of the family, my grandmother imparted many wonderful lessons to her kin, but the one I am most grateful for is the commitment to put *family first*. Unfortunately, sometimes it takes the loss of someone close to recognize the importance of family. In our society, family, both immediate and extended, often takes a backseat to our vocational ambitions. My grandmother's influence is evidenced by my father's strong devotion to our family. Growing up, I remember numerous times when my father had great opportunities for upward mobility within his corporation, but each and every time that would have required a move. My mother and father were emphatic about creating memories and establishing roots within a community. As a result, they sacrificed lucrative opportunities to remain in St. Louis. I am very grateful for their sacrifice. I know it must have been hard on my dad to watch his peers race past him on the corporate ladder, but for our family it was important to remain in St. Louis.

Each family is different, and in today's job market, transfers are often necessary, but one must always consider the costs. I have been wrestling with this same notion for many months now. The logical career step for me is to take a "higher" administrative position at a highly regarded school. I understand one must serve in certain roles in order to achieve other roles in which one may be able to serve better. At the same time, my wife and I hope to start a family soon. Regardless of my wife's willingness to move for my career, I know that when push comes to shove, at the birth of our first child, God willing, she will desire to be close to family. In the same way that my grandmother sacrificed for her children, my father did the same for my sister and me; and now it is my turn to make the best decision for our family, not necessarily what is best for me.

CAREER

I first entered the field of education because I felt as though it would be conducive to raising a family. Like most of us, it is easy to lose sight of what is truly important in life; one of the highest on that list is family. Society will not always understand the choices you make for your family, but I can think of no greater honor on one's deathbed than to be surrounded by family who love you, care for you, and admire you. I recently read a short paragraph in the local newspaper about a seventy-year-old man who was found dead in front of his running television set. His body had mummified because it was estimated he had been dead for over a year. The man had died of natural causes, and the police had only checked on him after his pipes burst. Reading this broke my heart. No one knew this man was dead for a year. No one cared for this man in his waning moments. In contrast, my grandmother was cared for, and her family knew within moments of her passing. My grandmother would be proud of the way her sons rallied around her during those last few months. It is no coincidence that all three sons were by her bed to say good-bye, even though two of the sons live miles away. Not all families are perfect, but most are a wonderful blessing that younger generations often take for granted. God orchestrates our lives for a reason. Think soberly when making vocational decisions that may pull you away from your family.

SEASONED ADVICE

Laurie Smith, thirty-five; Emmy Award nominee as Trading Spaces *designer;* Better Homes & Gardens *columnist; author of* Discovering Home; *Jackson, MS:*

I accepted Christ at a young age. Like many of us, I imagine, my faith life mirrors flying a kite. God is the kite. At times I would pull Him close, while other times I would allow Him to drift further away, but we were always connected. My story is one of grace. Early in life I was drawn to the stage but chose to give it up in high school. Eventually the theater called me back. While attending Southern Methodist University as a sophomore, a professor encouraged me to audition for the theater school. During the audition I was thrown an expected curve ball and I fell flat on my face; it had been too long. I had lost my edge. Instead I decided to pursue broadcast journalism. *At least I would still be in front of the camera*, I thought to myself.

I quickly rose to the top, garnering coveted internships, but I soon realized that I lacked the passion for the news that my peers wielded. My heart was pulled back to the arts. Through a series of connections, I landed a job with the Turner Network in Atlanta. While there I worked with actors promoting regional films. At first this role was exciting, but over time my frustration escalated. I did not want to talk to actors; I wanted to be an actress. *But I will never make it*, I thought to myself.

At twenty-seven and single, I felt as though I had missed my calling in life. One of my closest friends in Atlanta was an interior designer. She thought design would enable me to rechannel my creativity with a blank room as my canvas. After taking a few local classes and absolutely loving them, I convinced my father to help subsidize design school in New York. While in New York, I also signed up for theater classes in the village at night. Neither my design friends nor my theater friends understood me. Each group thought I was crazy. How on earth could those two fields enmesh? I did not know, but I felt the Lord's leading very clearly to pursue both fields. On numerous occasions I prayed for the Lord to remove this desire to perform from me, but it never happened. Through a whirlwind of events near the end of design school, I met my husband. Within eight months we were married, and I moved to Jackson, Mississippi.

Two weeks into my marriage, I was depressed. Newlyweds should be blissful, but instead I felt a huge loss in my life. In my mind, the performing chapter of my life was closed. Who would ever discover me in Jackson? Even though I landed a good design job in Jackson, something was missing. Everywhere I turned I felt extreme loss, culminating in Sunday school when I had to lead a discussion on "living the gap between what you dreamed and what you got." I was desperate. I pleaded with God to remove these yearnings from me. I wanted God to completely remove every morsel of desire. The next day I was numb. At work that morning I received a phone call from a designer friend in Atlanta. She apologized but told me she had given my name to a producer for TLC who desired to launch a design show with the crazy premise of working on two homes in two days for a thousand dollars or less.

Shaking, I fell out of my chair. Two minutes after hanging up the phone with my friend, the producer, Grace, called and eventually hired this crazy Southerner with red hair. One of the main reasons I was hired was because the execs wanted a designer who actually lived in the South. God orchestrated every one of my steps. Each stop on my journey has played a pivotal role in my development so I could be more useful to God. "Now faith is being sure of what we hope for and certain of what we do not see" (Hebrews 11:1). Never underestimate the power of merely trusting the Lord with every decision, no matter how crazy it might seem.

POINTS TO PONDER

1. Read 2 Timothy 1:1–14.

2. What are three of the most prominent characteristics you have inherited or learned from your mother's side of the family? Your father's side of the family?

3. Who inspires your faith the most, and why?

24

THE IMPORTANCE OF
BOUNDARIES AND BALANCE

I recently watched the Adam Sandler movie *Click*. This particular Sandler movie varies greatly in style and demeanor from many of its predecessors. Sure, there are many lowbrow humor jokes woven into the script, but the style and tempo of the movie are far more contemplative than the likes of *Billy Madison* or *Happy Gilmore*. The movie begins with Michael Newman (Sandler) desperately trying to climb his way up the corporate ladder only to find himself the recipient of countless broken promises from his unyielding boss. Early on the audience recognizes a trend in Newman's life—choosing work over family. One night at the apex of his desperation, he wanders into the back of a department store and encounters a crazy inventor who offers him the universal life remote. This remote gives its owner the ability to manipulate every situation. For instance, when Newman's wife is lecturing him, Newman merely presses Fast Forward. At first Newman loves the remote, but as his life quickly passes him by, he laments his decision. The remote exacerbates Newman's tendency to always choose work over family. Sandler's character serves as an excellent illustration of the importance of establishing boundaries and balance.

While writing this chapter, a freshman swimmer at Emory University was found dead at the bottom of the pool, President Gerald Ford died, and a colleague of mine had a heart attack and underwent triple bypass surgery. None of us knows when the good Lord will call us home. Life is precious. None of us knows how much time we have, but, barring any unforeseen catastrophes, "our problem is not too little time, but making better use of the time we have. Each of us has as much time as anyone else. The president of the United States has the same twenty-four hours as we. Others may surpass our abilities, influence, or money, but no one has more time."[1] How do you orchestrate your life? Let me suggest, much like Sandler's character, that the choices you make now and the boundaries you develop now regarding your career will help establish healthy patterns in your life for you and for your family. Here are a few suggestions to help you get started.

Prioritize. "Take control of each area in your life where He has given explicit instructions. When we bring our balancing problems to God, we discover that He never assigns us twice as much as we can possibly do. Instead, the Father shows us the appropriate priorities to use and then always provides whatever time and resources we need to accomplish His will."[2] At times it's difficult to determine which components of our lives hold the most worth. Rarely do the most important items scream for our attention the loudest—the neglected spouse, the child waiting to be picked up at practice, the elderly parent who hopes you'll take time out of your busy schedule to pick up the phone or stop by for a visit. All of us prioritize our lives, consciously or unconsciously.

Take an active role in how you manage your time. This may sound overly simplistic, but take care of those tasks that are the most important first. For instance, I do my best to begin each day in God's Word. For me, once my day begins, it's difficult at times to slow down. Like Jesus, "Paul selected his priorities with great care, allowing no time for endeavors that were not vital. His life demonstrated that strength of moral character develops through *rejection of the unimportant.*"[3] Once you have a clear picture of your priorities, establishing healthy boundaries helps you keep your top priorities at the top of your list.

Create boundaries. During my senior year in college I was interviewed for my business school newsletter. The interviewer asked me about my plans for the future. At the time I did not really have any explicit plans other than I had decided to pursue a career in education because the lifestyle would be more conducive for raising a family. For me, early on, being a dad and good husband were higher priorities than any chosen vocation. Andy Stanley, the lead pastor and founder of North Point Community Church (fifteen thousand members), decided early on in his "official" ministry that his family would remain his number one ministry. He did not just talk about it; he set up a healthy boundary by setting reasonable work hours so he would be home for dinner each night. What are your nonnegotiable items?

Say no. For Christians, saying no to people in need often proves daunting. But other people's crises are not necessarily your crises. Let me say that again: other people's crises are not necessarily your crises. "Our responsibility extends only to those things which lie within our control. Not every call for help is a call from God. It is manifestly impossible to respond to every appeal for aid. We must remember that circumstances beyond our control are no cause for self-accusation."[4] But obviously some calls for help do require our assistance. If your boss messes up and needs your help, in most cases your first responsibility is to honor your boss by assisting. Your boss probably would not appreciate you saying, "Your crises are not my crises." Staying in God's presence helps us ascertain whether interruptions are God-ordained or merely interruptions.

Devalue your own importance. Often the root of our inability to say no rests in our desire to feel important. Or we fear that if we say no too often, people will not need us. We have an incessant need to prove our worth to an organization or to others. As Rocky Balboa would say it, "I want to go the distance so I'll know I'm not a bum." Your worth comes from God and God alone. He has each of us on this earth for a reason and a purpose. In Philippians we see Jesus, the Son of God, choosing to humble Himself: "Who, being in very nature God, did not consider equality with God something to be grasped, but made himself nothing, taking the very nature of a servant, being made in human likeness" (Philippians 2:6–7). Jesus took on flesh to walk among us. Sinless, He willingly chose to humble Himself for us even though we are but specks in the hourglass of life.

Take a Sabbath. Rest. Re-create yourself. Give yourself the freedom to refuel your tanks. Recreation is key in order to stir the passions inside you. Down time allows your mind to wander. If every moment of your life is scheduled, there's no room for the Holy Spirit to lead you. For our scheduled society, "the Sabbath is a paradox. It is a day that requires great discipline to do nothing. Our efforts are focused on letting our guard down so that God can get to us. The reason we aren't given dominion over the seventh day is so that we can learn to let God achieve dominion over us."[5] In a sermon I once heard by Tim Keller, pastor of Redeemer Presbyterian Church in New York City, he suggested breaking one's Sabbath into three parts—avocation, contemplation, and inactivity (rest). In other words, one portion of your Sabbath would include activities that you enjoy and re-create your spirit, another would be reflective activities, and the third merely resting. Build a Sabbath into your normal week. Build a Sabbath into your career.

Unplug. With the advent of technology, truly resting is increasingly more difficult. We are accessible all of the time. In order to rest, you must be disciplined enough to unplug from technology. During swim season, my wife and I joined the team to attend the latest inspirational football movie. Not surprisingly my students were text messaging during the movie. But I must admit I was surprised when a few of them started answering their phones during the movie. "I'm sorry, I can't talk right now—I'm in a movie." So why did you answer the phone? Although I love technology, my spirit wrestles with purchasing the latest trend because I know that my desire for the latest and greatest will only grow with time. The invasion of technology will only continue to get worse. There are actually hotels now that will keep your Blackberry in a safe deposit box for you so you won't be tempted to use it. Set parameters for your life.

Give yourself a break. Inevitably with most of us, there will be seasons in our lives when overwork will be necessary in order to reach our goals. Whatever your season may be—perhaps school or starting your own business—navigating uncharted waters invariably requires more than the normal allotted times. Whenever I near a writing deadline, I warn my wife I will have to spend more time writing. When Tim Keller started Redeemer Presbyterian, he told his wife that the first three or four years would be extremely taxing, but then he would back off. As he tells it, after four years he came home from work one day to watch his wife smashing wedding plates. He had not kept his end of the bargain, and she was doing what she had to in order to gain his attention. Work hard, but also give yourself a break. Make sure you have others in your life who will keep you accountable to your allotted time frames for work and rest.

Reevaluate. "An unexamined life will drift toward imbalance. This is the way the modern world works. And an unbalanced life will not be kind to us in the area neglected. If God has instructed us to perform in a certain area—even at the decent minimum level—then we will not thrive if we disobey."[6] When I was more actively involved in theater, at the conclusion of every play we would have a postmortem. This served as an opportunity to discuss what went well with the play and what needed to be improved for future performances. In the same way, every so often in our lives we need to actively step back, actively unplug, and actively seek God's voice. What does God think? How are you doing? How can you more closely align with God's will for your life? Slow down and make the necessary changes. If you do not make the changes God wants you to make, He'll make them for you.

Your life will spin out of control if you do not guard against it. The world tells us that we need to create our worth, and for most of us that comes in the form of achieving "success" in our job. But our peers are not our standards. As Christians, we are held to a different set of standards. Each of us has a pre-set amount of time here on this earth. Fix your eyes on Christ (Hebrews 12:2), and let Him help you balance your time in order to give Him the most glory. He has a plan for you (Jeremiah 29:11) and will give you enough time to complete it. You will always have enough time for the things God intends for you.

SEASONED ADVICE

Dale Hanson Bourke, fifty-two; president of PDI; author and former editor of Today's Christian Woman *magazine; Washington DC:*

I started my own company when I was twenty-seven, which seems incredibly young to me now, but at the time I had an opportunity and my attitude was, *What do I have to lose?* It never occurred to me that I might be so successful that I would have employees, clients, and suppliers all depending on me at some point. So I went from being on a great adventure to suddenly being responsible for people and paychecks and delivering services. I was fortunate to have a great staff—mostly women—and I tried to be flexible with their hours so they could be with their families.

While I encouraged balance for my employees, I wasn't always so good at it myself. I loved to work, and I could easily get caught up in it. But when I was at home, I tried to be fully present for my family. I had my first son when I was twenty-nine, and I worked up until the day I went into labor and then brought him with me to the office a couple weeks later along with a baby-sitter—that was what was great about having my own company at the time. My second son was born four years later, and things began to get pretty hectic. When my children were in school, it wasn't always easy to plan business trips around last-minute school events, and I probably said "hurry up" to my sons far too many times. But they both say that they were proud of me for what I was doing and don't seem to have any long-term ill effects.

My sons grew up with a model of marriage that was very flexible. My husband often drove the boys to school on his way to work, and whoever got home first made dinner. The boys saw each of us contributing to the work at home and the family income. My older son mentioned the other day that he worries he will marry a woman who doesn't want to work and he'll be responsible to make enough money to support the family. He said he feels pressure to look for a job that is more about income than his passion. I think he sees now that a working woman can give her husband more flexibility in his career, and that seems like a very positive thing to him now that he is close to assuming that role.

My faith as a young woman was probably pretty consumer-like. I made deals with God. If He'd let me accomplish this, I'd do that. I'd pray for His intervention but rarely prayed just to experience His presence. When I lost a baby and a close friend and then my father within a short time, I was shocked. I suppose my life had gone so well that I didn't realize that tragedies happen to anyone and everyone. Somehow I thought I had immunity.

I suppose the essence of my faith now is that I realize it isn't all about me. I try to spend as much time as I can just experiencing God and recognizing His presence in the people and circumstances of every day. My faith is big enough now to see that day-to-day ups and downs aren't God giving favors or withholding His love. That's not how He works, and for the most part I lack the capacity to even recognize what He's about at the time.

Now that I'm in the second half of my life, I am less ambitious about success and more inclined to seek wisdom. I really am fine with letting God surprise me, a concept that terrified me when I was younger and had my five-year plans. When I look back, I see that I was fortunate to have several careers and perhaps will have more. I always tell my sons that they don't have to worry so much about what they will choose as their career because they will probably have more than one. Life is full of surprises. I try to embrace each day fully and spend less time worrying about the future. I see how frightening that concept is for my sons, but I try to remind them that it's like a distance race, not a sprint. The guys who had the fast start in a race too often ended up limping in toward the end of the pack. The winner was often a guy who started slow and paced himself. He ran his own race, not someone else's. God has a plan for each of us, and it doesn't often look like anyone else's or what we even anticipated when we were just getting started.

POINTS TO PONDER

1. Take a minute to write down the five most important areas of your life.

2. Next write down a boundary you could create in order to protect each area of your life.

3. Read Hebrews 4:9–11 and Luke 6:1–11.

4. How do those passages speak to you?

NOTES

1. J. Oswald Sanders, *Spiritual Leadership* (Chicago: Moody Press, 1994), p. 94.

2. Richard Swenson, *The Overload Syndrome* (Colorado Springs: NavPress, 1998), p. 71.

3. J. Oswald Sanders, *Dynamic Spiritual Leadership* (Grand Rapids, MI: Discovery House, 1999), p. 182.

4. Ibid., p. 184.

5. John C. Haughey, *Converting 9 to 5: A Spirituality of Daily Work* (New York: Crossroad Publishing, 1989), p. 47.

6. Swenson, *The Overload Syndrome*, p. 71.

In our 20s we make the most significant and formative decisions of our entire lives.

We decide what career to choose and whom to marry, how we will spend our money, where we will live, what type of people we will surround ourselves with, and generally what will be the guiding force(s) of our lives. Ironically, these choices are made at a time when the most wisdom is needed but the least is possessed.

As a 30-year-old Christian who has sought God's leading in making many of the above decisions, Colin Creel sets out to share both what he's learned as well as the advice of some older, wiser men and women who can look back with discernment on the life-molding decisions all twentysomethings face. By addressing such topics as romance, work, friendship, character development, and spiritual formation, PERSPECTIVES offers life-changing daily tidbits of wisdom for the searching Christian twentysomething.

Check out a FREE 15-week PDF Bible study at
www.colincreel.com/books.html